A Family Farm
Life on an Illinois Dairy Farm

Charlie Allison in typical
farm clothing, 1944.

A Family Farm
Life on an Illinois Dairy Farm

Robert L. Switzer

with an appendix by Frank E. Barmore

Published by the Center for American Places
at Columbia College Chicago

Published in 2012. First Edition.
Paper: 60# Glatfelter Offset

The Center for American Places
at Columbia College Chicago
600 South Michigan Avenue
Chicago, Illinois 60605-1996, U.S.A.
www.colum.edu/centerbooks

Printed in the United States by Maple Vail
Design by Brian Switzer, envision+
www.envisionplus.com
Set in DTL Documenta and ITC Franklin Gothic

Distributed by the University of Chicago Press
www.press.uchicago.edu

20 19 18 17 16 15 14 13 12   1 2 3 4 5

ISBN: 978-1-935195-34-4

For my grandparents, Charles and Mabel Allison,
and my parents, Stephen and Elva Allison Switzer,
who gave the best part of their lives to the farm.

Any book about family farming must now
not be romantic nor naïve, but brutally honest:
The American yeoman is doomed; his end is
part of an evolution of long duration.

Victor Davis Hanson,
Fields Without Dreams: Defending the Agrarian Ideal

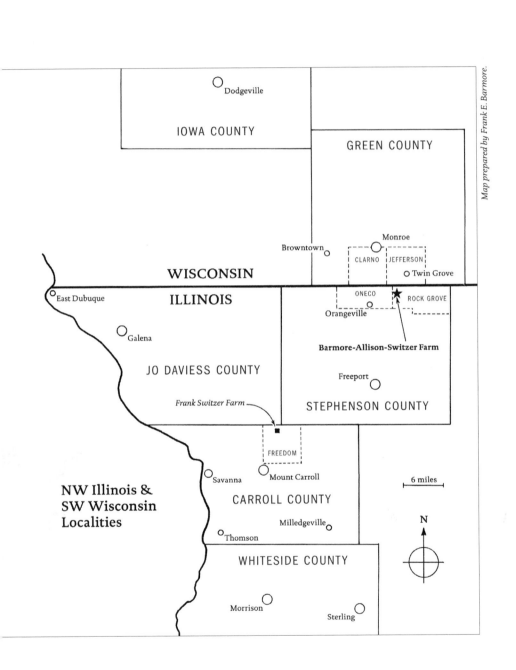

Dodgeville

IOWA COUNTY

GREEN COUNTY

Monroe

Browntown

CLARNO | JEFFERSON

Twin Grove

WISCONSIN

ONECO

ILLINOIS

East Dubuque

Orangeville

ROCK GROVE

Barmore-Allison-Switzer Farm

Galena

JO DAVIESS COUNTY

Freeport

Frank Switzer Farm

STEPHENSON COUNTY

FREEDOM

6 miles

Savanna

Mount Carroll

NW Illinois &
SW Wisconsin
Localities

CARROLL COUNTY

N

Milledgeville

Thomson

WHITESIDE COUNTY

Morrison

Sterling

Contents

Acknowledgments

This book is dedicated to the memory of my maternal grandparents, Charles and Mabel Allison, and my parents, Stephen and Elva Allison Switzer. The story of our farm is primarily their story, and it is their lives that are unsparingly examined in this book. My life, so full of blessings, was built on a foundation of their labor and love. They deserve honor and respect.

This book is not only the story of a family farm; it is truly a family document. It is to my immediate family that I must express my deepest gratitude. Our son Brian created the woodcut prints in the book and wrote sections of chapters 5 and 6. Brian first urged me to begin writing on nonscientific topics because he wanted to work together with me on a project. This book is the first fruit of his encouragement. I am delighted that Brian is the graphic designer for this book. My wife Bonnie provided not only the watercolor paintings of the farm that appear in this book, but inspiration, encouragement, and love. Bonnie's mid-life emergence as an artist taught me the valuable lesson that I might become something other than a biochemist in retirement. Our daughter Stephanie contributed the beautiful remembrance in chapter 6; her family and Brian's family provide happy assurance that our family's story will continue into a fifth shining generation. My brother Steve and his wife Dorleen provided recollections and corrections that have enriched the narrative. I am grateful for Steve's supportive contributions, even if this book is not as he would have written it. My narrative contains more autobiographical elements than I intended when I first began to write it. Scott Turow expressed well the inevitability of this at the conclusion of his novel, *Ordinary Heroes*: "When we tell our parents' tales to the world, or even to ourselves, the story is always our own."

I thank our neighbor and friend, Professor John A. Jakle, for first introducing me to the Center for American Places. Very special thanks go to Susan Arritt, a series editor for the Center for American Places' My Kind of series. Susan's contributions went far beyond her fine editorial work for this book; her enthusiasm, encouragement, and thoughtful suggestions were not only crucial to the evolution of the manuscript into its final form, but created a lasting, cherished friendship. I thank Anne Sanow for her thorough and sensitive copyediting of the final manuscript. Dorothy Loudermilk deserves special thanks for her cheerful and expert preparation of high-quality digital copies of the original materials for the book's many illustrations and assistance in their assembly into publishable form. I am grateful for the support and enthusiasm of George Thompson, the founder and former director of the Center for American Places at Columbia College Chicago during the development and approval of the manuscript. Brandy Savarese and Jason Stauter of Columbia College Chicago provided invaluable professional assistance during the later stages of editing, design, and production; it was a pleasure to work with them.

Many thanks to our friends Bob and Judy Jones, Ted and Audrey Brown, Rick and Linda Troy, and Clark McPhail for encouragement when this book was in manuscript and its novice author wavered; to Frank E. Barmore, great grandson of N. J. Barmore, who built the house and barn on our farm in the 1860s, for his very thorough research into Barmore family history and the architecture of the farm buildings, which is described in the appendix to this book; to Don and Joyce Bates for kindly inviting me to tour and photograph the restored house and outbuildings on our former family farm; to Vicki Otte, clerk and recorder of Stephenson County, Illinois, and her colleague, Deb Hartman, for valuable assistance in researching the history of transfers of deeds to the family farm; and, finally, to librarians at the superb libraries at the University of Illinois and the Urbana Free Library for friendly and able assistance with research.

Aerial view of the
Allison-Switzer farm
in 1987.

Prologue

One hundred years ago, American agriculture was very different than today's agriculture: the family farm was at its center. In 1900, 42 percent of the U.S. population lived on farms; by 1990 that number had dwindled to less than two percent, and more than half of these families obtained a substantial portion of their income from off-the-farm employment.[1] There were 6.4 million farms in the United States in 1910; in 1987 only 2.1 million farms remained.[2] Remarkably, most of this decline occurred between 1950 and 1975.[3] The average American farm in 1900 consisted of 124 acres. More than 90 percent of farms had fewer than 260 acres.[4] These farms were typically operated by a man and his wife, their children, and often a few members of their extended family, such as parents or unmarried brothers or sisters. Farm families were generally large ones. The family farm's sources of power, beyond simple human labor, consisted of a team or two of horses and perhaps a windmill to pump water. Enormous steel-wheeled steam engines—which more closely resembled the steam rail locomotives of the time than modern tractors—were used for threshing grain, but only one farmer in twenty owned a steam engine during the peak period of their use in agriculture.[5]

By the end of the twentieth century the average American farm had grown to 461 acres and farms of more than a thousand acres were common.[6] Technological advances brought about a great increase in agricultural productivity, but they also required modern farmers to adopt an economic mode akin to the manufacturing industry. Modern agriculture increasingly required major capital investments in large and expensive machinery and buildings, hybrid and genetically engineered seed, commercial fertilizers, herbicides, and pesticides. Such large investments meant that individual farmers had to work ever-larger farms. Farmers also became much more specialized. Gone were the days of raising a few cows, hogs, and chickens and feeding them with grain and hay grown entirely on the farm. Agriculture evolved toward the corporate "factory farm" we know today—very large land areas are cultivated and thousands of animals are raised by highly organized corporations, and few of the employees are members of a single family.

A consequence of this revolution in American agriculture has been the disappearance of hundreds of thousands of small family-operated farms. As these small farms were absorbed into much larger, more economically viable units, the families who lived on them moved to towns and cities and found new ways to support themselves. Any drive through rural America will provide abundant (though often mute) evidence of this change in the form of weathered, windowless abandoned farmsteads. The corn and soybean rows come close to the old barnyards; some of the sheds and corncribs may still be used, but the cost of clearing the site doesn't justify the bit of additional field that would be gained.

The disappearance of so many small single-family farms and the way of life they supported can be understood in technological, sociological, and economic terms, and this book briefly summarizes such trends as part of its narrative. However, a statistical approach does not enliven the individual family stories that accompanied these changes. Each abandoned farm was the stage for a personal and emotional drama that was played out there, very often a drama of frustration and loss. The gaunt gray buildings witnessed these dramas, but they stand silent. This book is the personal story of one such family farm from the different perspectives of four generations. It is the story of modest dreams and frequent disappointments; a story of sturdy independence and hard physical labor; loss and remembrance; a story of love unspoken or whose expression was postponed too long. It is the story of my family's farm and thus the story of many farm families.

The Allison-Switzer farm was located in Stephenson County in northwestern Illinois, at the western boundary of Rock Grove Township about a mile south of the Illinois–Wisconsin border and five miles northeast of the village of Orangeville (see map, p. 8). My family owned the 121-acre farm from 1916 to 1991, a period of seventy-five years—the period of radical transformation just described. My maternal grandparents, Charles and Mabel Allison, operated the farm from 1916 to 1946. They retired to a little house in Monroe, Wisconsin shortly after my parents, Stephen and Elva Allison Switzer, took over the farm in the summer of 1946. I would turn six years old that summer; my brother Stephen A., called "Allison" or "Al" in those days, was eight. Although my brother and I left the farm in the late 1950s, my parents operated the farm and lived in the big old house for the rest of their lives. My mother died in January 1977; my father in September 1991. Early the following year my brother and I, joint heirs, sold the farm, and its cultivatable land was incorporated into a large farm adjoining it.

In this book I aim to bring the players in this story to life, to depict the settings where they lived and worked, and to capture the essence of a time gone by. I use the voices of the family members themselves, along with photographs, documents, and artwork created by my wife Bonnie and our son Brian, who was also the graphic designer for this book. My father wrote a large section of chapter 3; Brian and our daughter Stephanie wrote portions of chapters 5 and 6. This is a collaborative family effort in the way that working the land together once was.

This is not a "history," but a memoir. I have attempted to place my family's farm into the broader context of trends in farm economics and farm life throughout the twentieth century, but the characters in this story are not statistical stick figures illustrating the decline of a midwestern family farm. They are my family. They would *not* have been pleased by the frank intimacy with which I have told their story. I intend no disrespect in doing so, and I hope that my deep affection and understanding will be evident. However, it would not be accurate to write a sentimental history with unhappy elements expunged. Their lives were often very hard, and that harshness extracted a high physical and emotional cost. In that, their story may be typical of life on a family farm during those years. The details of their lives provide an intimate portrait of a once common way of life, now almost entirely vanished from the American countryside.

Elva on her grandparent's
farm around 1910.

Chapter One

Charlie and Mabel and Elva (1916–1937)

By the time I formed my first memories of my grandparents, from 1946 onward, they seemed rather old and exhausted to me, worn out by years of hard work and living under harsh conditions. Grandma Mabel was painfully thin and short of breath, often stopping and sighing. She had lost most of a lung to tuberculosis years earlier, but as Grandpa Charlie said with pride, "she could work like a man." She wore her gray hair in a severe bun at the back of her head and preferred loosely fitting dresses in gray or lavender. She had a long thin face and rarely smiled. I don't believe that she was a happy person—life had been hard, the rewards and joys few. Formidable as she was, it was difficult to feel close to her, although she was fond of her grandsons and occasionally expressed her affection by inviting us to take a lemon drop or a mint from a glass candy dish on a Victorian sideboard. She spoke of the thirty years that she and Grandpa had operated the Orangeville farm with a mixture of pride and resignation, as though it were a mountain climbed or a prison sentence served in full. "Thirty years!" she would pronounce, as though that said all that was needed.

Grandpa Charlie had a full head of white hair and a white handlebar mustache. He was almost always dressed in a blue chambray work shirt that was buttoned up at the neck and sleeves, blue denim overalls, and heavy leather work shoes. When he went out to do the chores, he added a blue denim jacket and a droopy, well-worn felt hat with a hand-braided horsehair hatband, and low rubber boots. His pockets contained objects that fascinated us: a large, silver "turnip" watch, a worn but very sharp pocket-knife, and a shiny golden brown horse chestnut, which he claimed protected him against rheumatism. Grandpa Charlie was slightly stooped and moved slowly, using a wooden stockman's cane in later years, but enjoyed better health than Mabel. Both had lost all of their teeth. Grandma had a set of false teeth that occasionally clicked and disturbed her speech, but Grandpa refused to replace his lost teeth. This caused his cheeks to appear somewhat sunken, but the effect was largely hidden by his luxuriant mustache. His toothless condition forced him to gum his food, cut by Grandma into small bites. Once in a while he would choke on his food—not a coughing, spluttering, and red-faced choking, but a condition that caused him to make frequent hiccupping sounds, which always caused consternation and irritation in his wife. He also suffered from a quasi-narcolepsy, which he attributed to a severe heat stroke he had suffered as a teenager while working in the fields on his father's farm. He would fall asleep in his chair quite abruptly and awake calmly a few minutes later. This often occurred at mealtimes, causing my brother and me to titter. The condition had much affected his life. He had been forced to drop out of high school, where his lapses into sleep were not tolerated. He could operate horse-drawn machinery and drive a team and wagon, but he tended to fall asleep driving a buggy on smoother roads, and he never learned to drive an automobile for fear of falling asleep at the wheel. Thus, in 1946, the Allison farm was stuck in the nineteenth century: all of the machinery was horse-powered, and there were no automobiles or tractors on the farm. His narcolepsy had condemned this intelligent and creative (if rather dreamy and impractical) man to a life of manual labor.

Like many farmers and workingmen of his time, Grandpa had a hernia (which he referred to as a "rupture"), the result of an old injury, aggravated by heavy lifting. Years later, my father would have a similar hernia surgically repaired, but Grandpa adopted a simple palliative of the time: a truss. This contraption of leather straps and pads worn under his clothing must have been hot and uncomfortable, but he rarely spoke of it. "Keeps my guts in," he commented dryly.

Although he didn't express it verbally, Grandpa was obviously very fond of his grandsons. He had a knack for including us in his work, which often involved repairs or simple carpentry. He made us feel that we were a useful part of the job. He taught us skills and entertained us with stories as we worked. (My mother shared this ability, but, unfortunately, my father, who was the primary taskmaster on the farm, lacked it.) Grandpa's activities were often more fun than practical. He taught us how to carve whistles from thin willow sticks in the spring when the flow of the sap made it easy to slip the bark as an intact cylinder off of the pale rubbery wood underneath. Grandpa took us fishing in nearby creeks using simple poles and earthworms as bait. We caught more crayfish than edible fish, but the outings were welcome breaks from farm chores, calm and companionable times with our grandfather.

On a warm Sunday afternoon in 1946, just before my brother and I were to start attending the nearby one-room country grade school on the southwest corner of our farm, Grandpa took us on a long hike to collect walnuts and butternuts from wild trees whose locations he knew around the neighboring farms. We trampled off the thick green pulpy outer husks to expose the woody shells of the nuts and gathered them into a burlap or "gunny" sack. In the process our hands were thoroughly stained with the dark brown juice from the husks. Grandma was furious. "Charlie," she fumed, "Just look at those boys! That'll never wash off. They'll have to go to school tomorrow looking like wild Indians!"

Although the big old farmhouse was certainly large enough for the six of us, there were strains of which I was only dimly aware at the time. In late 1946 or 1947 my grandparents moved to Monroe, Wisconsin, to live a quiet and frugal retirement. Grandpa set up a shop in the basement and filled it and the garage with junk. He worked in a small workshop owned by a distant relative. Grandma's health declined and in early 1953 she died of congestive heart failure, her heart long overburdened by the loss of her lung, while my mother, my brother, and I sat miserably in an adjacent room. Grandpa Charlie watched without tears as the undertaker removed his wife's withered body. "She was down to skin and bones," he said sadly.

Grandpa lived on alone for another eleven years in the little Monroe house. These were years of contentment. Charlie enjoyed company, but he was comfortable with solitude. He puttered in his basement shop and worked part-time in his relative's shop. He developed circulatory problems in his legs, which led to severe swelling and open ulcerations. The ulcerations were often aggravated by Grandpa's attempts to treat them with home remedies that included bag balm (a greasy ointment used to treat sores on cow's udders), bacon fat, and kerosene. On a few occasions he required hospitalization, followed by lengthy convalescence with us on the farm. I remember these times with great fondness, because he told so many stories about his travels out west or in California sometime in the period between 1902 and 1905. He had gone there in search of work and adventure and, as he told an interviewer for the *Rockford Morning Star* in 1962, "my girl (Mabel) was in the eighth grade and I had to wait until she growed up." His stories gave a fascinating glimpse of a vanished world not far removed from the Wild West of American legend. "Wonderful city," he told me once of Phoenix, Arizona. "All wooden sidewalks everywhere. You didn't have to walk in the mud." He told the *Morning Star* reporter that when he'd been in Los Angeles, "I could have bought acres and acres of land for $25, but, golleys, it was sand and sagebrush. Who'd want anything like that?" As I grew older, he added stories he hadn't deemed suitable for younger children—stories of houses of ill repute, of a Chinese cook urinating into the biscuit dough to make it rise, of a fatal shooting he witnessed in Needles, California. California was forever inscribed in my imagination as a magical place. Charlie's vision grew dimmed by cataracts, which in the early 1960s weren't considered correctable. Never fond of shaving, he grew a thick white beard and delighted neighborhood children by putting on a red jacket and cap and giving out candy, pretending to be Santa Claus.

I was home from graduate school in California—where else could it have been?—for a short visit in the summer of 1964 when my mother and I dropped in on Grandpa and discovered that his legs were in terrible condition again. His physician insisted on another hospitalization for treatment. This time Grandpa was very reluctant to go to the hospital, having a premonition that he would not leave it alive. "Don't ever get old, Bobby," he said to me tearfully. "It's a terrible thing." Given Grandpa's resilience we had no strong reason to expect a fatal outcome, but within a week or two he developed pneumonia, fell into a coma and died. He was eighty-seven years old.

* * * * *

Charlie and Mabel Allison weren't always old and physically exhausted, of course. When they purchased the farm near Orangeville in 1916, they were young and must have viewed the prospect of owning their own farm with optimism and pride. The thirty years that lay before them appeared quite differently from the way Grandma saw them in 1946.

The period from 1900 to 1920 was one of exceptional growth in prosperity for American farmers, so much so that it has been called the "golden age of American Agriculture."[1] The value per acre of farm crops increased by 73 percent from 1899 to 1909, while the cost of items farmers purchased increased by only 12 percent.[2] From 1910 to 1920 alone the average annual gross income of farms more than doubled from $1,155 to $2,467.[3] The advent of World War I in 1914 provided an additional powerful stimulus for agricultural prices and production. Although the average cost of farmland more than doubled from 1900 to 1910, Charlie and Mabel Allison were among many who felt the time was ripe to buy their own farm.[4]

Charles H. Allison was born in 1877 near Milledgeville, Illinois. He was a grandson of Fisher Allison, an original settler in the area, who had emigrated from England via Canada. Fisher Allison combined farming, the operation of a mill, and his calling as a Methodist circuit-riding preacher. Grandpa claimed that his family farm had served as a station on the Underground Railroad. Four of his uncles were veterans of the Civil War. One, Joseph F. Allison, was wounded twice in action and another, John H. Allison, died in the Union Army in 1862 ("killed by the falling of a tree," states the ornate but mouse-chewed muster of Company G of the 39th Infantry Regiment of the Illinois Veteran Volunteers, leaving us one hundred and fifty years later to wonder exactly how the young man's life ended.) It was a reasonably well-educated family. Charlie's father, C. Wesley Allison, was a farmer and businessman. He was active in local politics and an ardent reader. Charlie's mother died quite young, and he did not get along with his stepmother.

The sunstroke that induced Charlie's lifelong narcolepsy abruptly ended his education. While still in his teens he quarreled violently with his father, "knocked the old man down with a single tree," as he told us, and left home for good. He lived with relatives in northern Illinois and worked as a farm laborer in the area and in southern Wisconsin. Some time during that period he met a slender dark-haired girl with snapping dark eyes, Mabel Campbell, from rural Green County, Wisconsin. Mabel was the second oldest of four children of Millard F. and Delila (Whitehead) Campbell (a fifth child, a son, was born much later.) Curiously, Mabel was the only one of the siblings to marry when she came of suitable age (although her brother Everett married very late in life after a decades-long engagement and the death of his spinster sisters). Aunt Maude, Aunt Esther, and Uncle Everett were all familiar figures at family gatherings (the younger brother had died horribly at seventeen years of age from peritonitis resulting from a ruptured appendix). Mabel was deemed too young to marry by her parents, so Charlie took off for his adventures out West. A photograph taken during those years shows a handsome man with thick black hair and fine dark mustache. He isn't smiling, but his dark eyes shine with confidence and a hint of mischief. Charlie and Mabel were married on February 15, 1906 after his return. The framed wedding certificate hung on the wall in their bedroom at the time of Charlie's death, legitimizing in the eyes of the Victorian world their long occupancy of the same bed.

The young couple operated several different farms near Dodgeville, Wisconsin, sometimes for cash rent and sometimes "on the halves," which meant that half of the proceeds from the sale of milk, livestock, and crops were given to the owner of the land as rent. This was a common arrangement at the time for farmers who had not inherited their land.[5] On March 8, 1907, Charlie and Mabel's only child, my future mother Elva Delila Allison, was born on the Dodgeville farm. Grandma later reported disgustedly that the attending physician had been drunk. There was little security or opportunity for advancement in operating a rented farm, and most farm couples yearned to own their own land. Charlie's frustration is expressed in a letter he wrote to his father on April 12, 1913, shortly after a move to a new rental farm:

Dear Father,

I received your letter some time ago and have been so very very busy moving that I don't hardly know what way to turn.

I am straight north of Browntown about two ½ miles till you come to the end of the road and the buildings are wright turn. on the place known as the Iverson Farm or near the Miere Cheese factory . . . [After discussing the possibility of buying a farm, Charlie continues wearily.]

I rented on the halves this time . . . My I am getting so tired of fixing up place after place then just move off and let some one else have the benefit of my work. . . . I don't believe I am going to like this half business at all. . . .

The years of World War I brought improved earnings and optimism to Charlie and Mabel. They bought the 121-acre farm northeast of Orangeville, Illinois, from Elmer and Anna Denny in March of 1916 for $16,335, a very large sum at the time—more than twenty times the average annual income of a full-time factory worker. This was the farm that I refer to as the Allison-Switzer farm. The price of $135 an acre reflected the optimism of farmers in the early twentieth century, but it would impose a burden of debt that was to weigh heavily on Charlie and Mabel for many years to come.[6]

The newly acquired farm was part of a larger tract of land (a quarter section, 160 acres) deeded by the State of Illinois to Levi, Daniel, and Elizabeth Starr in 1844–1845, during the period of rapid settlement of northwestern Illinois that followed the Blackhawk Wars and the end of conflict with the Indians in that area. In 1858, Nathaniel Jennings Barmore purchased 120 acres that included part of the Allison-Switzer farm and later added sizeable tracts of adjacent land to the farm. In about 1867, Barmore built the house and barn that still stand today; his farmstead was the original home of the family. In subsequent years Barmore divided his holdings into three parts, retaining for himself and his wife the 121 acres that was to become the Allison-Switzer farm. Farm buildings were erected for his descendants on the two other portions. In the late 1940s these farms were still operated by his grandsons, F. Glenn Barmore to the east and Jennings Cahoon to the south (see the appendix to this book written by Frank E. Barmore, a great grandson of N. J. Barmore.)

The farmhouse was quite large and had clearly been modified over the years. At one time two families, who lived separately, evidently occupied it, because there remained two sets of stairs to the second floor, one of which was later floored over at the top and served as an odd little closet. We were told by Jennings Cahoon that a second kitchen was attached to the house on the east side, but that it had been detached and moved south to his farm house, where it served as a summer kitchen until torn down in the 1950s. The house was an attractive structure with white clapboard siding and green louvered shutters framing its many windows, served by three chimneys. Two porches graced its south side, one recessed at the front of the western half of the house and a small decorative porch that projected out in front of the eastern half of the house, opening onto a parlor that was largely unused in Charlie and Mabel's time. Wooden gingerbread decorated the eaves of both porches and the vertical supports of the little porch.

The house was much larger than was needed by a family of three. The five upstairs rooms were used primarily for storage, although one or two were furnished as bedrooms. The upstairs was unheated in the winter, except for what little heat might escape from the stovepipes that passed through from the stoves below on their way to the chimneys, which began on the second floor. The stovepipes passed through decorative round iron grates with moveable louvers to regulate the amount of warm air rising to the upstairs rooms. The cool rooms were ideal for storing cured hams and bacon and dried fruit; they were permeated by a rich, smoky aroma. The parlor was furnished, but was only open in warm weather; Charlie and Mabel kept its ill-fitting doors tightly closed and packed with rags in winter.

As was typical of farmhouses in 1916, the house had no modern utilities. Although most cities and larger towns in the United States had electrical and telephone service before 1920, few farms had them before the late 1930s, when they were electrified, largely with support of the Rural Electrification Administration.[7] In 1935, the first year for which the REA reported data, only 11.1

percent of farms had electricity.[8] Kerosene lamps and candles provided light. An ornate coal-burning potbellied stove heated the big front room on the west side of the house, and a large kitchen range, fueled by both wood and coal, served for cooking, hot water, and heat in the kitchen on the north side of the house. The other rooms were unheated except for such heat as might diffuse into them. The house was not insulated. The windows were drafty and covered with frost on the inside in winter. A stove also stood in the parlor, but it was rarely used. The only islands of warmth during the long cold winter months were the living room stove and the kitchen range; the little family surely spent much of that season close to them.

Charlie and Mabel carried water from a well, which was located sixty feet west of the house. An outdoor wooden privy served the family's sanitary needs—a cold dark trip on a snowy winter night, if chamber pots were not used. I remember the privy well. It was a "three-holer" with wooden trap doors to cover the holes, which came in three sizes—big, medium, and small—like the three bears. Baths required water heated on the kitchen range and were an infrequent luxury in winter in spite of the family's daily immersion in the dirt and smelly manure of the cow barn, hog house, and chicken house. In the summer a large galvanized tub full of water was left outside to warm in the sunshine, providing a welcome bath to remove the dust and chaff of fieldwork.

A large garden and orchard lay to the east of the house, which supplied the family with virtually all of the fruit, vegetables, and potatoes that, together with farm-grown meat, milk, and eggs, formed the family's diet. A nearby cheese maker bought the milk from the farm and sold cheese and butter to the family. Little food was purchased off the farm, except for flour, sugar, salt, and spices.

Like their neighbors, Charlie and Mabel were dairy farmers.

Milk was their most important cash crop. Thus, the most important farm building was the barn. (This has remained true for dairy farmers. My mother often ruefully pointed out that the farmers in the area invested huge sums in large modern dairy barns and milking parlors while neglecting the century-old farm houses where their families lived.) Nathaniel Barmore erected the barn on the Allison farm in about 1867. It was a typical Pennsylvania bank barn, a rectangular box of solid post and beam construction with a simple gable roof.[9] It was set into a hillside so that a team and wagon could enter the upper level hayloft (always called a "haymow" by my family) by driving up an inclined ramp through tall roller-mounted doors. The ground floor walls were constructed from local stone, but the rest of the barn was of wood frame construction. Four 40-foot-long wooden beams supported the frame and heavy wooden planks that formed the floor of the haymow, which was also the ceiling of the cow barn below. These beams were simply the trunks of four tall trees with two sides roughly cut flat with an adz and the bark remaining on the other two sides. The framing or "bents" was constructed with smaller timbers of sawed lumber and larger rough-hewn braces and beams assembled in a mortise-and-tenon fashion in which sawed segments on the ends were fitted into holes in cross members and secured with wooden pegs. Vertically placed sawed boards, perforated at intervals with many louvered windows to permit airflow into the haymow, made up the barn's siding. Wooden shingles covered the roof. The nails used to secure the sides and shingles were flat nails, not the round wire nails used by later generations.

Originally, in the lower level of the barn a series of wooden stalls arranged in parallel rows perpendicular to the long axis of the barn housed the cattle and horses. The livestock entered the barn through a series of double doors along the south wall and faced one another to eat from common mangers. Probably this south entry wall was recessed by about six feet under the upper structure in the original barn, so that an "overshot loft" sheltered the entry (fore-bay) area. The farmer moved behind the animals in parallel alleyways to milk the cows, bed the stalls, and carry the manure out the south doors. Some time before Charlie and Mabel bought the farm, either the Barmores, or more likely the Dennys in the 1911–1916 period, converted the lower level of the barn to a floor plan that arranged sixteen iron cattle stanchions in two rows facing away from a central concrete driveway along the long axis of the barn. They cut large doors into the stone walls at each end of the barn to permit the animals to enter and allow passage of a horse-drawn manure spreader through the barn. This made for less laborious cleaning of the barn and fewer steps during milking and feeding. The old doors to the south were closed up, and the wall was moved out to remove the overshot loft, but a series of windows in the new wall allowed light from the southern sun to enter. Sturdy wooden stalls and mangers for horses were constructed on both sides of the driveway at the east end of the barn. Some of these served as pens for calves in the winter and as a stall for a bull.

The haymow level of the barn was much taller than the lower cattle level. Wooden grain bins lined one side of the barn floor, and a large hay storage area lay on the other side of a central driveway. Probably in the original use of barns of this design, grain was threshed by trampling the grain on the central barn floor, and the straw was lifted with forks, leaving the grain and chaff on the floor. Wind blowing through the grain assisted in winnowing the grain from the chaff, and the grain was then shoveled into the adjacent grain bins. By Charlie and Mabel's time, however, a large mobile threshing machine powered by a steam engine via a long, thick pulley belt threshed the grain outside of the barn. The thresher blew the loose straw into a stack just outside the barn for use for bedding for the cattle in winter, and the grain was hauled up to the barn floor by wagon and shoveled into the bins by hand. Loose hay—that is, hay that was not baled—filled the haymow in the upper level of the barn.

The barn was unheated in the winter, but stuffing of the cracks in the large doors at the ends with gunnysacks kept the barn relatively free of drafts. It received significant warmth from the bodies of the cattle and the fermentation of the manure pack in the stalls. Charlie and Mabel pitched hay down from the cold upper mow through small chutes, which they kept closed with trap-doors when not in use. The barn was hardly cozy in winter; it was chilly at best with temperatures around freezing or lower during the coldest winter days. When Charlie and Mabel let the cattle out to drink or opened the barn doors to admit the manure spreader for cleaning, the temperature dropped sharply. By contrast, in summer when the end doors were open wide and the cattle were only in the barn at milking time, the barn could be a miserably hot, sticky, stinking place. Flies tormented the cattle and Charlie and Mabel as they sat on wooden stools (simple Ts made of two perpendicular plank segments nailed together) and leaned into the cows' hot flanks to milk them by hand. Countless times Charlie and Mabel received the stinging lash of a urine-soaked or dung-encrusted tail in the face or were kicked sharply by an irritable cow.

This was the setting in which my grandparents labored through the cyclic routines of their lives. The daily rhythm of milking the cows in the early morning and again in the evening never varied. Feeding the cattle grain and hay, refreshing the animals' bedding, and cleaning the barn added to the daily chores in winter. In summer the cattle were out to pasture, so the barn chores were easier, but fieldwork filled the long summer days. Charlie and Mabel kept a flock of chickens, which had free run of the barnyard, and a small herd of hogs, which they fed and watered daily. While Charlie saw to these chores, Mabel prepared meals over the kitchen range, did the laundry, and cared for the house. She also had primary responsibility for the large garden and the canning of fruit and vegetables.

The only surviving letter in my possession written by Mabel is to her sister Esther, dated August 12, 1917. It reflects her preoccupation with the work of the farm:

We have the piece of grain by the church [no longer standing, but at that time located next to the one-room school] cut and shocked and the other one is about half cut, but not shocked. The blackberries are so slow ripening. I canned one qt. and made a couple pies. The grasshoppers eat them so bad. I don't mean the pies, the berries! I wish you had some of these apples I don't know what to do with. My chickens are better. I lost 56 the week you went home and 10 since. I got some dope to put in their water. I lost two ducks in that rain Tuesday and have one cripple. Edna and Porter [Charlie's younger sister and brother-in-law] *and two kids came Tues. evening and stayed over night. . . . I was in the field shocking oats when they came.*

The annual cycles of crop farming added much additional labor to the daily barnyard routines.[10] A rapid snowmelt usually signaled the arrival of spring. The farm buildings were situated at the bottom of a broad shallow east-west valley, so when the heavy snow pack melted from the surrounding fields, a gushing stream flowed past the buildings though a waterway and eroded into ditches at points just south of the buildings. At times the water was so deep that it was difficult for a team and wagon to cross. On cold nights the water froze into a rough, irregular stream of ice. A second, smaller stream of snowmelt flowed from fields to the north, creating a barrier between the house and the barn to the west. Traffic churned the areas near the buildings into mud. Charlie hauled in rocks and gravel in an attempt to solidify the muddy barnyard, but his efforts were largely ineffective.

A city dweller might imagine the first fieldwork in the spring to be plowing, but it actually was the much less pleasant task of hauling the winter's accumulation of manure onto the fields. Often the snow was too deep in winter to permit Charlie to haul the day's horse and cow manure from the barn and scatter it on the fields with a horse-drawn spreader. So he and Mabel scooped it out of the barn and piled it in a large pile just west of the barn. The winter's dung and bedding also remained in the hog houses and the chicken house until spring. When the snow and mud permitted it, Charlie pitched load after load by hand into the spreader and hauled it with the team to the fields. Large rear wheels drove a conveyer belt that slowly moved the manure to the rear of the spreader box, where whirling blades scattered it behind as the team hauled the spreader along.[11] The manure fell in brown stripes across the fields to be plowed into the soil as fertilizer. The process attracted flocks of birds scavenging through the manure for edible bits of undigested corn.

Another mythic image of the nineteenth-century farm is the single moldboard plow mounted below a V-shaped frame with two long curved handles. A team of horses (or mules or oxen) pulled the plow, and the farmer walked behind it controlling the depth and direction of the furrow with his strong arms on the handles. A frequent and unpleasant experience for the plowman was the rough jolt received by his body when the plow struck a subsurface stone, of which there are many in northwestern Illinois fields. I saw just such a plow among the unused farm implements on the farm when I was a boy, and no doubt Charlie plowed many acres with it. However, he later plowed with a gang plow in which two moldboard blades (or "bottoms," so this was a "two-bottom" plow) were mounted below a heavy iron frame. Charlie rode on the plow on an iron seat and controlled the furrow depth with levers. The greater effort of plowing two furrows at a time required a three- or four-horse team.

It was not remarkable that Charlie and Mabel did not own a tractor and did all of their field work with horse-powered implements. Early gasoline-powered tractors were heavy, unreliable, and expensive. A few farmers bought tractors during the prosperous years of World War I, but in 1920 only 3.6 percent of U.S. farmers owned tractors.[12] The introduction in 1924 of the Farmall by International Harvester, which was adapted for use with row crops, led to increased use of tractors on smaller family farms, but by 1930 only 30 percent of Illinois and Iowa farms owned them.[13] Most farmers were desperately cash-poor during the 1920s and 1930s; mortgage payments, taxes, and other essentials left little over for the purchase of modern farm machinery. Charlie and Mabel continued to farm with horses until 1946.

Charlie and Mabel had more than half of their tillable land in pasture and hay for the dairy herd and less than a quarter each in corn and grain, usually oats or barley. The first farmers in northern Illinois grew the same crops, usually corn, year after year in the most productive fields. This led to soil erosion and loss of fertility, so the farmers were persuaded by research results from agricultural colleges to rotate the crops: corn, then grain, then hay for one or more years, then repeat.[14] Charlie prepared the newly plowed ground for planting by disking and harrowing, first planting the grain and then the corn, which is more sensitive to late frost. The most difficult plowing was the cutting of established sod from the hay fields to return them to corn. Some areas on Charlie and Mabel's farm were too hilly and stony for good crop farming, so they remained in permanent pasture.

Altogether Charlie plowed, disked and harrowed, and planted to grain or corn some forty to fifty acres every spring. He did this alone with a team of horses and horse-drawn implements. Forty acres is about the area of thirty-six football fields—a daunting task for a man to face every spring for thirty years! Working in good weather for eight hours a day, one man and a team of horses could plow forty acres in ten days. Disking required five additional days, two and a half days to harrow, and three more days to plant the forty acres in corn, if the weather was good.[15]

Charlie sowed grain with a horse-drawn drill. He mixed the grain seed with seed for hay that grew slowly in its first year under the rapidly growing "mother crop" of oats or barley. Thus, he grew and harvested grain in the first year, and established a crop of hay for the following year in the same field. The corn was planted in twin straight rows, so that spacing between the rows permitted removal of weeds with a cultivator whose wheels were of the correct width to avoid crushing the young corn plants. Charlie set the planter to drop its hills of seed at regular intervals by passing the planter through a long wire with repeated knots spaced at the distance between hills. He stretched this wire across the entire length of the field and moved it manually at the end of each transit with the planter. The reason for dropping the hills at such regular intervals was to make the spacing between them the same from both directions. Charlie could plow out the weeds between the rows with a cultivator, then repeat the process after turning his cultivator at a right angle to the original direction. The use of herbicides to control weeds or pesticides to ward off insect-borne grubs and worms was unknown. Charlie applied no fertilizer other than previously plowed-down manure. Removing weeds used a cultivator, a horse-drawn apparatus in which twin sets of small blades plowed up the earth on both sides of the cornrows. Charlie rode the rig and steered the blades with both his hands and feet. When the corn plants were very small, it was necessary to cultivate slowly to avoid uprooting or covering them. Cultivating forty acres of corn in this way required approximately three weeks' labor.[16] Moving at such a slow pace with his eyes on the cornrows below him, Charlie occasionally turned up Indian arrowheads and spear points. He had a handsome collection to show his grandsons by the 1940s.

Like all of his fellow farmers at the time, Charlie simply used a portion of the previous year's harvest for seed. Development of high-yield, disease and insect-resistant hybrid corn varieties began early in the twentieth century, but commercially produced hybrid seed corn did not come into general use until the 1930s and 1940s.[17] However, Charlie was slow to adopt expensive innovations. Later, when it became clear that large gains in productivity resulted from use of hybrid seed and commercial fertilizers, especially with corn, my father began using them in the 1940s.

Charlie and Mabel completed the plowing, preparation of the seedbed, and planting phase of the annual cycle by late May or early June, depending on the year's weather. Then they began harvesting: first hay, then grain, perhaps a second cutting of hay, and finally corn in the late fall. Hay was cut with a horse-drawn mower whose wheels drove the chattering sickle blade whose teeth reciprocated rapidly against a stationary blade in the cutter bar that extended to the side of the mower. When the hay had dried in the swaths in which it fell, Charlie or Mabel raked it into heaps for harvest. Originally, they used a dump rake, which was essentially a broad two-wheeled axle supporting a row of large, parallel curved steel teeth behind it. These dragged the hay into a heap, which the driver of the team riding the rake dumped into mounds when he tripped a lever to raise the set of teeth. The sweating couple loaded the heaps of dry hay onto a broad flat-bottomed hay wagon by hand with pitchforks and hauled it to the barn. They pitched some of the hay into the haymow directly from the wagon, but most of the time Charlie used a team of horses hitched to an arrangement of pulleys and a large steel-tined harpoon fork to haul a large mass of hay up and along a steel track mounted under the peak of the barn roof. Flexible teeth in the fork dropped the hay into position in the haymow when they pulled a rope that moved the teeth so as to free the hay. Even with this convenience, Charlie had to distribute the hay in the stifling hot haymow with a pitchfork, because simply allowing it to heap where it fell in mounds below the track didn't permit the entire haymow to be filled.

Later Charlie replaced the dump rake with a side-delivery rake, which permitted collecting the dried hay much more rapidly into long continuous windrows. Use of a mechanical hayloader made picking up the hay from the windrows less laborious. The hayloader was a large device with a long flat metal surface that inclined up and toward the back. A series of ingeniously designed oscillating bars with wire fingers worked above the flat surface. A rotating cylinder of wire fingers scooped the hay up from the windrows and fed it onto the inclined sheet. The oscillating finger bars moved the hay up the incline and dumped it onto a trailing hay wagon. Mabel drove the team that pulled the loader and wagon over the windrows. The turning wheels provided the energy needed to power the cylinder and oscillating bars. Charlie stood on the hay wagon with a pitchfork and moved the hay about to collect a full load. Contemporary methods of harvesting hay by baling it or by chopping and blowing it into wagons did not appear in northern Illinois until the 1930s and later.

Charlie and Mabel harvested their hay alone or by taking turns with a neighboring farmer, but threshing the grain was a communal activity involving an entire ring of neighboring farmers. Few farmers could afford to buy their own threshing machine and steam engine or early gasoline tractor needed to power it. A wealthy farmer or a contractor generally owned this equipment and moved it from farm to farm. A ring of cooperating farmers, each providing his labor and a wagon and team of horses, brought the grain to the thresher rapidly. A single long day completed the job on most farms. A speedy harvest was much desired. Each farmer had previously cut and bundled his grain into sheaves with a "binder," an updated version of the famous McCormick reaper. The farmers stacked the sheaves by hand into piles called "shocks" to complete the drying of the grain and to keep it dry. If the threshing was delayed too long, much of the grain could be lost. If the weather was rainy and the grain couldn't dry properly, it would become moldy. If the weather was dry and the threshing too long delayed, the brittle straw lost its grip on the grain and many kernels fell to the ground and were lost.

Charlie and Mabel could look forward to threshing as a lively social event. Harvesting the shocks and feeding the thresher was hot, dusty work, but the farmers generally enjoyed working together, shouting out encouragement and mock insults. The younger men competed to show who could work the hardest and fastest. Mabel's day was consumed with preparing a huge mid-day meal for the participating workers: potatoes and gravy, fried chicken, ham or beef, fresh vegetables from the garden, freshly baked bread or rolls. Most of the farmers did not drink alcoholic beverages, at least during the day, but they drank fresh milk, coffee, iced tea, and lemonade in large quantities. The big tables were noisy with storytelling, laughter, and the sounds of consumption. Practical jokes were common. A favorite was to pass the butter to a neighbor at the table, quickly twisting the dish at the last moment so that his thumb plunged into the soft butter. After loading their stomachs so heavily, many of the dusty, overall-clad farmers sprawled on the grass under the big trees around the house for a half hour or so to allow digestion to get under way. Then they returned to their work until the shocks of grain were threshed or darkness ended the work. The ring moved from farm to farm until they had harvested all of its members' grain. In sunny dry weather this required two or three weeks. If the weather was rainy, much longer times were needed, and those farmers whose grain was threshed last had moldy grain and straw as a bitter reward for their labor.

Grain harvest in northern Illinois occurred during July and August. Afterward, except for a likely second cutting of hay, which was usually of lower yield than the first, Charlie and Mabel had a respite from fieldwork until the corn harvest in the fall. Many farmers collected a portion of their corn for silage while the stalks were still green and the ears were immature. There was a wooden silo on the north side of Charlie and Mabel's barn, and they prepared silage in some years, but Charlie complained that his chopped corn tended to get moldy, and he abandoned its use. Eventually the empty silo blew down in a windstorm. Charlie sawed the staves into shorter segments, which he used to build four distinctive round hog houses. My father used these strange round buildings throughout his years of raising hogs, but they eventually fell into ruin when he stopped using them.

When the fields of corn turned dry and golden brown in October, harvest began. Charlie cut most of the corn with a corn binder, which cut and collected the stalks into bundles, loosely wrapped with twine. A group of bundles was collected on an apron of iron fingers and dropped together at intervals in the field. Later the bundles were collected by hand and were erected into corn shocks. These teepee-like structures required some skill to assemble, for they had to remain upright throughout the winds of winter. Charlie used a team and wagon (or sled in deep snow) to collect a few shocks at a time and bring them to the barnyard, where he husked the corn and used the fodder for cattle bedding (and a bit of low-quality feed). I recall vividly collecting corn shocks in winter from my boyhood; they became homes for a variety of field mice, moles, and even opossums and raccoons, which scurried in panic in all directions when we destroyed their snug winter nests. By spring, all of the corn shocks had been re-moved from the fields.

If Charlie wished to harvest the ears of corn to be ground into cattle feed or to sell all at once, he picked the ears by hand, one or two rows at a time, using a husking pin to assist peeling the husks from the ears. He threw the ears into a wagon with high sideboards on the opposite side that was slowly pulled along by a team of horses. Like most farmers, Charlie stored the ears of corn in a slatted corncrib near the barn. He left the fodder in the field and simply ran over it with the team when he picked the next rows. It was a slow job to pick a 10- or 15-acre field of corn this way; it has been estimated that a month and a half was required for one man and a team of horses to pick forty acres.[18] Charlie and Mabel often picked corn together. Cattle grazed the fodder in a fully picked field in winter if the weather permitted, but it was lean rations for them. Charlie emptied each wagonload of ears of corn by hand, shoveling it into the crib.

Each day of hard work in the fields began and ended with barn chores: milking the cows by hand, feeding the hogs and chickens, and gathering eggs. A windmill, later supplemented with a large one-cylinder McCormick-Deering gasoline engine with a heavy iron flywheel, pumped water for the cattle, but Charlie hauled water to the hogs and chickens in pails or old milk cans. Charlie and Mabel filtered and collected the milk in 10-gallon milk cans, and cooled the cans by immersing them in cold fresh well water in the same tank from which the cows drank. The Barmores (or possibly the Dennys) installed an underground pipe to carry water from the well to a concrete tank by the barn, but this eventually leaked so badly that Charlie rigged up a system of V-shaped wooden troughs sealed with tar at the bottom through which the water flowed to the tank, a typical low-tech solution. The troughs tended to leak when the summer sun dried the tar, however, and Charlie had to move them every time he wanted to cross their path with a horse and wagon.

Charlie hauled the day's milk with a spring wagon every morning to a cheese factory located about a mile east of the farm. The horses trudged wearily to the cheese factory, but ran most of the way home, knowing that their morning meal awaited them. A vivid memory from 1946 or 1947 is the team running out of control down the lane and into a field on the way back from the factory, while Charlie shouted in anger and empty milk cans flew off the wagon. My brother, then nine years old, had accompanied his grandfather to the cheese factory and got the ride of his life. No one was hurt, but Mabel, who witnessed the incident, was frightened and angry with Charlie.

Most of the neighboring farmers brought their milk to the cheese factory too. Delivery of the milk was a popular daily social contact for the farmers, who exchanged news, gossip, and complaints about the weather and their crops when they met to deliver their milk. The cheese maker weighed and pasteurized the milk and paid each farmer in proportion to the amount delivered when he sold the cheese, usually big wheels of Swiss cheese. The cheese factory used the Babcock test to determine an average butterfat content for each farmer's milk. (The Babcock test measures the butterfat content of milk by digesting milk proteins with hot sulfuric acid; a floating layer of fat is then separated in a centrifuge and measured in a calibrated flask.) The factory paid a differential for milk of higher butterfat content, because they used a cream separator to remove the cream in excess of 3 percent and sold it for butter. Charlie and Mabel kept as much of their milk as they needed for themselves and skimmed cream from the top of the milk every morning. In their early years on the farm, they made their own butter in a hand-cranked glass churn with wooden paddles. Whey from the cheese-making process accumulated every day in a big tank at the cheese factory; when transported back to the farms and mixed with ground oats, it made a sour-smelling but nutritious swill for the pigs—and a magnet for flies in summer.

Mabel shared milking and barnyard chores with Charlie and worked with him in the fields many times, but her chores went well beyond that. She had full responsibility for cooking, washing, cleaning the house, sewing and mending, and, during the summer months, tending a large garden and canning the fruit and vegetables from the garden and orchard.[19] The orchard contained perhaps a dozen apple trees, including some varieties rarely seen today such as Wolf River and Yellow Transparent. Charlie planted a pear tree and several plum and cherry trees as well. Laundry was an all-day, once a week task. Mabel carried water from the well and heated it on the kitchen range. She scrubbed the clothes with a washboard in a large tub, rinsed them in another tub, and fed them through a hand-cranked wringer. She hung the wet clothes on outdoors clotheslines to dry summer and winter, although in bitter winter she hung them indoors on wooden racks. The work clothes—filthy with cow and pig dung or dirty and greasy from fieldwork—Mabel washed last, after the indoor clothing and underwear.

During the summer months Mabel moved her operation from the southern portion of the kitchen, which connected to the rest of the house, to the unheated northern half, the summer kitchen (also called the "wash house" because the laundry was done there). There was no fire in the kitchen range. Instead, Mabel did her cooking and canning on a kerosene-fueled stove, which produced more controllable and less extraneous heat. Preserving the summer's harvest of vegetables and fruit by cooking it in large quantities and sealing it under vacuum in glass jars provided near-ly all of the family's supply of these foods for the winter months. Mabel's garden and canning chores were a major preoccupation from May or June until the fall frost. An interesting detail in the kitchen was a connection between the summer kitchen and the winter kitchen via a wood box built into the wall separating them. Charlie stored wood in the wood box by lifting a trapdoor in the summer kitchen and dropping it into the box. Inside, in the winter kitchen Mabel lifted a similar trapdoor to retrieve the wood in winter without going out into the cold summer kitchen. However, a lot of cold air entered the kitchen through the wood box.

In spite of the cold and long dark winter, Charlie and Mabel welcomed the relief from fieldwork. The rhythm of twice-daily milking and barn chores, meals and laundry continued, of course, but there was also time for more personal pursuits: reading and sewing for Mabel, carving and woodworking for Charlie. Charlie's peculiar tendency to fall asleep while sitting prevented him from much reading.

Bitterly cold, snowy winters alternated with hot, humid summers, punctuated by many bright sunny and refreshing days. A farmer learns to accept whatever weather comes his way. In the Midwest that includes violent thunderstorms in the summer and occasional tornados. The nearest approach of a devastating tornado of which I am aware was on June 22, 1944. I was not on the farm, but my older brother was staying with our grandparents there when the tornado approached, and he vividly remembers being hustled into the farmhouse basement by Grandma Mabel. The family farm was spared, but a path of devastation cut through nearby farms. Two people and hundreds of farm animals were killed, and many buildings were obliterated.[20]

Thus, Charlie and Mabel's years slipped by—years of hard work and frequent discomfort, years in which they passed from young to old, lost their teeth, grew gray and gaunt, stooped and arthritic. It does not appear to have been a happy marriage. Charlie was inclined to putter and dream, not particularly ambitious or interested in labor-saving innovations. Mabel voiced her frustration freely. My mother reported that Mabel was something of a nag and a scold, but she worked very hard under uncomfortable conditions and lived a meager life. Added to the usual hardships of farm life of the period was a twenty-year siege of extreme financial stress.

Charlie and Mabel were involved only to a limited degree with the affairs of the nation and world. They read newspapers and magazines, including *National Geographic*, which collected in great, fascinating piles in an unused upstairs room. But the outside world, especially the world of agricultural economics, intruded forcefully into their lives. The high farm prices prevailing during their first four years as farm owners collapsed in 1920 and throughout 1921. From June 1920 to May 1921, the average price of ten leading U. S. agricultural products fell by two-thirds.[21] Prices for Charlie and Mabel's farm products—corn, cream, eggs, and hogs—decreased to their lowest in 1921–23 to 23, 44, 27, and 30 percent, respectively, compared to their 1919 high values.[22] Increased crop acreage, stimulated by the previous years of high demand and prices, combined with exceptionally favorable weather, led to farm production that outran demand. Farmers suddenly found themselves producing surpluses that were driving them into bankruptcy. Although farm prices recovered somewhat by 1923, the entire decade was one of acute economic stress for most farmers. Farmland values declined steadily by 2 to 5 percent per year from 1925 to 1929.[23] The indebtedness acquired by farmers during the "golden years" now bore down heavily: in 1910 farm mortgage debt was 10 percent of total land value, and by 1928 it had increased to 22 percent.[24] Forced sales from foreclosures on mortgages and failure to pay taxes soared from around 1,000 per year in the 1915–1920 period to a peak of nearly 8,000 in 1925; there were more than 5,000 forced sales per year throughout 1923 to 1928.[25]

The Great Depression of the 1930s—which clearly had begun for American farmers long before the stock market crash of 1929—brought even lower agricultural prices and added misery. Of commodities that Charlie and Mabel sold, the average price farmers received for corn dropped from 77 to 32 cents per bushel between 1929 and 1932; the price of hogs fell from $12.93 to $6.13 per hundredweight. Overall, by 1932, average American farm incomes had declined to 40 percent of their already-depressed

1929 level.[26] Charlie and Mabel could subsist on their garden and animals to a great extent, but they had to buy certain food staples, clothing and farm equipment, and to pay taxes and make mortgage payments. Their cash income from sales of milk, hogs, and eggs sank so low that they had great difficulty in paying the interest on their farm mortgage and real estate taxes on the farm. Payment on the mortgage principal was out of the question. More than once Charlie scrambled among his relatives and acquaintances seeking to borrow enough to prevent foreclosure.

Little detail survives from those miserable years. I recall Grandma Mabel bitterly telling the story of a consignment of hogs sold in Orangeville, shipped by rail to the Chicago stockyards, where they found no buyer for several days. The total of shipping and stockyard fees nearly equaled the proceeds of the sale. "We might as well have shot them right here!" she exclaimed angrily years later. "At least we'd have had the meat." Charlie, who had a more calm, fatalistic view of life, said almost nothing about the Depression years, but he must have suffered too.

I do not know exactly how Charlie and Mabel escaped losing their farm. Possibly, the Emergency Banking Act of 1933 provided relief, because closed banks couldn't foreclose on mortgages. Some cash came to the family from the settlement of Charlie's father's estate in 1942, and from sales of gravel to build local roads from a pit that Charlie and Mabel reluctantly opened on the farm. Ultimately, they were rescued from their burdensome mortgage by the high farm prices and inflation brought by World War II. Seeking to stimulate agricultural productivity during the war, Congress passed laws in 1941 removing restrictions on production and guaranteeing farm commodity prices at 85 percent of their levels during the "golden years" of 1910–14, and further raised the support level to 110 percent in 1943.[27] Net U.S. farm income rose from $2.3 billion in 1940 to $9.2 billion in 1945.[28] Nearly thirty years after they bought the farm, Charlie and Mabel finally owned it, but they were exhausted by the effort.

* * * * *

From the point of view of their farm economy, Charlie and Mabel were unfortunate in another way: they had only one child and that child was a girl—my mother, Elva. Farm families with sons had a ready source of free labor, starting when the boys were six or seven years old. A farmer with multiple sons could manage larger herds, more acres of land, and harvest his crops in a timely manner. Farm girls were given many household, garden, and barnyard chores, but they generally did not work in the fields with their fathers. (There were exceptions, of course, especially when the girls were fully grown, and many farm wives worked in the fields, as Mabel did.) The following account by Mark Friedberger gives a picture of the workload on a farm like Charlie and Mabel's and the value of family labor:

In general, no farm families worked harder than those in the hog-dairy enterprise. In the 1930s it was calculated that in northeast Iowa the total labor on a farm was the equivalent of about two men working nine hours per day all year around. The operator provided half of this labor and the rest of the family furnished approximately 23 percent of it. [Domestic and garden chores were not included in the total farm labor.] Hired men were often used from March to October. [Charlie and Mabel did not hire outside help.] Farmers usually worked an average of 12½ hours per day from May to November, and even in January they toiled 8½ hours a day. The dairy was the heaviest user of labor throughout the year, especially in the winter, when five or six hours [per day] were needed for chores . . . one milk cow required twenty-two minutes a day of labor. [29]

My mother was nine years old when her family moved to the Orangeville farm. She assumed the usual duties of a farm daughter, but was too small and thin to do hard fieldwork. Mabel taught her what she knew of cooking, canning, gardening, and sewing, although Mother always said that Mabel was impatient and short-tempered with her, stating that it was "easier to do it myself" than to tolerate young Elva's novice mistakes. It was a relationship that did much to undermine Elva's sense of self-confidence and self-sufficiency. She savored her solitary moments, which came frequently because she had no siblings. She became fond of sewing, embroidery, and reading. She proved to be an outstanding scholar and excelled in her studies at the one-room country grade school that stood on the southwest corner of the Allison farm. A single teacher taught all eight elementary grades. Elva walked the modest distance to and from school until she completed eighth grade in 1921

Pleasant Hill School was typical of the 10,613 one-room rural and village schools found in Illinois in 1917.[30] Illinois had embarked on a program of upgrading its rural one-room schools and provided detailed standards for doing so. Teachers were required to have completed four years of high school and were to be paid a salary of at least $40 per month. Even specifications for school wells and outdoor toilets were provided. In 1914, none of the schools in Stephenson County (where Pleasant Hill School was located) met these standards; by 1917, fifty-seven of the county's 125 one-room schools were certified as complying with state requirements.[31]

When the time came for Elva to attend the high school in

Orangeville, her family decided that the only practical decision was for her to board with a family in the village. For Elva to travel the five miles each way to and from Orangeville every day was not feasible. In winter the roads were filled with snow; in spring they became impassable tracks of deep mud and ruts. The family did not own an automobile, and Elva probably could not have reliably gotten one to Orangeville because of the bad roads. The Allisons also did not have an extra team of horses that Elva could take to Orangeville and keep in a livery stable during the school day. Arrangements were made for Elva to live with the Frautschy family, who lived on the upper floor of their grocery store on Main Street in Orangeville. The Frautschys had children of high school age, and Elva found the family to be very congenial. She was quick to learn how to assist in the store. She happily settled into fours years in Orangeville (except during the summers, when she lived on the farm). She continued her outstanding scholarship in high school, and although she was somewhat introverted, she formed lifelong friendships with a few of her classmates. In 1925 she graduated from Orangeville High School as the valedictorian of her class. Elva's high school curriculum included English, mathematics, biology, history and Latin. She was especially fond of biology and Latin, and chose these subjects later in college. (Latin was still a standard part of a high school education in the 1920s. A generation earlier, Grandpa Charlie related, the esteem placed on Latin was so high that the valedictorian of Milledgeville High School gave his oration in Latin, to frustrated calls of "talk English!" from uncomprehending members of the audience). Photographs from 1925 show Elva to have been a small, attractive girl with carefully waved dark hair and intense, intelligent, very dark eyes. It is the face of a serious, somewhat shy girl, who formed strong friendships, but only slowly and more easily with other intelligent girls.

Her high school class of 1925 had only fifteen graduates, eleven boys and four girls.

After graduation from high school Elva had little desire to return to the farm, and no romantic attachment likely to lead to marriage had developed. So she decided to become an elementary school teacher, like Miss Grace Coomber, who had been her favorite teacher at Pleasant Hill School. She qualified for an elementary teaching certificate by examination during her senior year in high school, followed by six weeks in normal school at DeKalb, Illinois (which eventually became Northern Illinois University) during the summer of 1925. Elva took up her first teaching position in a rural one-room elementary school not far from Orangeville in the fall of 1925. She had responsibility for all classes for all eight grades, just as her teacher had had at Pleasant High School. She bought and learned to drive a used Model T Ford coupe to drive to school, and she lived at home on the farm with her parents. The Model T was still stored, disused, in a garage on the farm when my brother and I were boys. It was in good condition, except for some deterioration in the felt upholstery. We loved to play in it. In the early 1950s as we learned to drive tractors and farm trucks, we persuaded my Dad to get it started and we drove it around for fun. Ultimately, Dad sold it to some neighbor teenagers, who quickly ran it into the ground—a pity, because it would have become a valuable antique car if it had been properly preserved.

My mother was a very well-organized and conscientious teacher, and she was warm, protective and motherly with her younger pupils. Probably she found it more difficult to establish adequate discipline with the older boys, quiet and gentle as she was, but I do not recall her ever speaking of problems.

Elva taught elementary school for one year, but yearned for a higher education. Her educational ambitions were unusual in a rural farm girl; as late as 1940, only 2.8 percent of rural youth of age twenty-five or older had completed four years of college, and only 10.3 percent had completed four years of high school.[32] In 1930, only 46 percent of Illinois farm boys and 55 percent of farm girls aged sixteen or seventeen were attending school.[33] In the fall of 1926, Elva traveled by train to Carthage, a small town in west central Illinois that was notorious as the site of the jail where Joseph Smith, the founder of Mormonism, had been murdered by a mob many years earlier. Carthage was also the site of a small liberal arts college associated with the Lutheran Church.[34] I do not know how Elva came to choose Carthage College. Her family was not Lutheran, and, although she attended religious services, took a few required courses in religion, and grew fond of sacred music while at Carthage, she never joined the Lutheran (or any other) church. Possibly she chose the college because it offered a partial scholarship to students who graduated at the top of their high school class. Whatever the basis for the choice, it was a good one. Carthage was small enough for the shy young woman to become comfortable and find friends, and she received plenty of attention from her professors, all the more so because she was a serious and gifted student. She continued her studies in Latin and added classical Greek.

After a year, however, finances forced Elva to discontinue her studies. The costs of tuition, books, and room and board made it impossible for the struggling Allison family to support her college expenses, and her savings from her meager teacher's salary were exhausted. She returned to Orangeville and took another position as an elementary school teacher. In 1928, Elva's college ambitions were revived when her Aunt Olive and Uncle Lee Doty (Olive was Charlie's younger sister) generously offered to help with expenses. Lee Doty was a prosperous Chicago banker. Olive had received a college education and cherished it. She recognized a kindred spirit in her bookish niece and chose to provide her with this dreamed-of opportunity.

Elva resumed her studies at Carthage in the fall of 1928 and completed the remaining three years without interruption. She added an intensive program in biology to her major in Latin and Greek. Her biology professor, Professor Alice L. Kibbe, became an important role model for her. Kibbe was a pioneer: an eccentric but much-loved professor whose extensive collections still can be seen in the Kibbe-Hancock Heritage Museum in Carthage. Very few women had earned the Ph.D. degree and achieved the rank of professor, even at a small church-supported college without an expectation of ongoing original research, in the 1920s. Professor Kibbe took a strong interest in her bright young protégé; Elva's admiration for her mentor was unbounded. Years later, I was to absorb from my mother the feeling that nothing could lead to a more wonderful life than to become a professor in a college or university, an ambition I clearly took to heart. Mother saved her textbooks and many fascinating glass-topped sample boxes filled with shells and carefully dissected, dried, mounted, and labeled animals and plants, and boxes of preserved microscope slides, some specimens preserved in formaldehyde and sealed with wax in glass bottles. These intriguing objects were kept in a trunk in an upstairs bedroom. When I reached an appropriate age, I was allowed to examine and study these treasures. Biology, viewed from this somewhat old-fashioned perspective, was generously mixed with the real thing for me, played out by the wild birds and animals, the domestic animals, and the abundant plant life on the farm. What could be more fascinating? Today, in my seventies, I continue my lifelong love of the study of living creatures. Many of Elva's biological specimens were donated to Orangeville High

School after I was grown, but a few remain in the family's collection of memorabilia.

When Elva was a junior at Carthage College she met a tall, muscular freshman with dreamy blue eyes, a sensuous lower lip and fine light-brown hair. He was Stephen Switzer from Mt. Carroll, Illinois, and he was destined to become her husband for forty years and my father. They must have seemed an unlikely couple: she was small and dark, shy and scholarly; he was large and fair, no scholar by his own testimony, unworldly, but charming and outgoing. He was four years younger than she, and her friends teased her about "robbing the cradle" when they began to see one another regularly. They formed an enduring friendship that led to marriage seven years later. The economic hardships of the Depression prevented an earlier marriage. Dad dropped out of college after only one year and struggled to establish himself, as he describes in his own words in the next chapter.

Elva graduated from Carthage College in 1931 with excellent grades. She had earned a high school teacher's certificate, but she was unable to find a job—any job that used her education, any job at all. She applied for elementary teaching positions no more advanced than the one-room school she had abandoned three years earlier. One evening she traveled a considerable distance to be interviewed by the school board of a small rural district, only to note that some of the school board members, who were tired farmers, fell asleep during her unsuccessful interview. She was forced to return to her parents' farm, discouraged and humiliated. Mabel was furious with the "waste of time and money" spent on Elva's college education, which was proven to her satisfaction by the futility of Elva's search for employment.

While a senior at Carthage College, Elva was awarded a partial scholarship to pursue graduate study at Cornell University, probably because of the support of Professor Kibbe, who had earned her Ph.D. there. Cornell was and remains an outstanding research center in the biological sciences. It is fascinating to speculate how her life might have developed if she had been able to accept this opportunity. A graduate scholarship did not pay the full expenses of graduate school in those days, however; research students were even expected to buy their own equipment and research materials. Few women were encouraged to pursue graduate degrees or research careers. Indeed, many schools discouraged women applicants to graduate school or refused them altogether. Elva had no heart to ask her Aunt Olive and Uncle Lee for yet more financial support. Her parents were opposed to further education. After all, what had been gained from Elva's bachelor's degree? So she declined the scholarship, and a fond dream died.

Around this time Elva's grandfather, C. Wesley Allison, who was in his eighties and living alone after the death of his second wife Jenny, became a cause of worry for Charlie and his sister Olive. It was proposed that Elva might repay Olive and Lee Doty for their support of her college expenses by living with the old man and serving as his housekeeper-companion. Elva was fond of her grandfather, although she did not know him well, and the prospect of living in his pleasant big old house in Milledgeville, Illinois—away from her nagging mother and dreamy father—appealed to her. Also attractive was the fact that her college boyfriend, Stephen Switzer, lived not far from Milledgeville. Their courtship continued, and eventually they agreed to marry. They felt that they should wait until they could better afford to do so, but in the mid-1930s the rural economy became, if anything, even worse than before (as Stephen has so vividly detailed in the next chapter). By February of 1937 they gave up: they still couldn't afford to marry, but they did so anyway. Standing together in the parlor of the Lutheran parsonage in Milledgeville, they were joined as husband and wife. The witnesses were my father's sister Helen and Kenneth Whitney (Helen's future husband), who later confirmed my mother's story that Dad had been three hours late for the ceremony. After the brief ritual the pastor, M. D. Kilver, rolled up the little rug they had been standing on and gave it to the newlywed couple. It was one of their few possessions.

59   Charlie and Mabel and Elva

Dad home on leave
from the Navy with my
brother, then called
Allison, left, and me on
the Allison farm in 1944.

Chapter Two

Stephen's Story (1920–1946)

In a sense I tricked my father into writing this fragment of an autobiography. He had often complained that most historians had a biased view of the Great Depression. He claimed that they concentrated on the urban situation and ignored the conditions experienced by farmers. He felt that their pro-Roosevelt bias led the historians to credit the New Deal with ending the Depression, a view he rejected. He argued that the Depression grew worse for farmers and rural communities throughout the 1930s and that only the stimulus of war production at the outset of World War II ended it.[1]

I urged him to write his own history of the Depression. I knew that he was not in a position to write a real history. I hoped he would write his own personal story, and so he did. This was a man who liked to read and talk, who had many and strong opinions, but who revealed little of his personal feelings. I hoped that he would expose a little more of himself and that this writing enterprise would draw us closer to one another. That was only successful to a limited extent, but Dad left the fascinating document from which I have extracted this chapter. As he got under way, Dad warmed to the task and even wondered whether his words might someday find publication. He mailed his first install-ment to me in February of 1985, and sent several additional seg-ments at irregular intervals. In March 1986, he abruptly ceased writing without giving a reason. He never wrote another installment.

Dad wrote these fragments of his life story under difficult circumstances. By the 1980s he was living alone on the farm. His knees were severely arthritic, destroyed by years of squatting un-der dairy cows and other hard farm labor. Worse, macular degen-eration had severely dimmed his eyesight. He could read only large print. He wrote his chapters in longhand, but he could not read or correct what he had written. Sometimes the words ran off the page entirely; a few were undecipherable. I was used to read-ing his (never very legible) scrawl, so I carefully transcribed each letter as I received it. Although I have edited the letters for clarity and to construct a narrative focusing on my father's personal ex-periences, I have allowed my father to tell his story in his own words. It provides a vivid picture of life in rural Illinois in the 1920s and 1930s.

* * * * *

I do not know how many generations of my family before me have been farmers. I am certain of at least three, and since I have spent almost all of my life living on farms or engaged in farm-related occupations, my opinions are from a farmer's viewpoint.

During World War I, American farms became rather sud-denly prosperous because of world demand for their products. My father, who had begun farming some five years previously, was able to upgrade his equipment and also bought his first car the year the United States entered the war, 1917.

As farmers and other kinds of entrepreneurs have always done, a little prosperity encouraged them to expand. A couple of years after the close of the war, when Europe was again able to become self-sustaining, prices of farm commodities fell, and many farmers found themselves trying to pay off debts incurred in the expectation of better prices. The technology to improve production that is now available had not yet become well known, (if it existed) at all. Also, farmers were very slow to adopt new methods in agriculture.

My parents bought a farm in 1922. The previous owner had lost it to the mortgage holder. He seems to have been something of a ne'er-do-well, but we were to learn that the deck had been stacked against him. As I remember, the price was $17,000 for two hundred acres. My folks had $1,000 to pay as a down payment and then took a first mortgage at 6 percent and a second mortgage at 7 percent. (Like the Allison family, Dad's parents chose an unfortunate time to buy a farm. Illinois farmland prices rose by 60 percent from 1915 to 1920, but fell to one-third of their 1920 value by 1933 and did not recover their full 1920 prices until 1950).[2]

My father seems to have had the idea that one ought to have a farm with "wood and water." These things were in abundance. The water was really no problem. There were many springs and at the source they never froze. The wood was something else. We went into the woods with crosscut saw, ax, wedges, and a maul. A good man in good timber could probably cut a cord (128 cubic feet) in an ordinary day. Often the procedure was to take the trunk (butt cut) and cut and split it into fence posts and to use the top, limbs, etc. for firewood. That was done, that is, if the tree were of a durable wood, such as white or burr oak. After the wood was reduced to logs up to ten or twelve feet long, it was hauled and piled to be later cut into lengths short enough for a stove by use of a portable "buzz" or circular saw. The saws were usually mounted on a wagon and powered by a one-cylinder gasoline engine. The large chunks were split with an axe for use in the kitchen stove.

It seems apparent that Dad did not realize that soil is the most important part of a farm. At any rate, in the area where I grew up the land was not very productive, and because of its rolling character, it was subject to heavy erosion. The better land had heavier mortgages, so if production was greater, so were the costs.

I don't wish to suggest that subsistence farming was not viable in the 1920s. We raised vegetables, canned and stored them, and slaughtered animals, and cured and canned the meat. So the cash expended for food was for flour, sugar, salt, and condiments mainly. Gasoline was used for the Model T Ford and for gasoline lamps and lanterns. In the summer we used kerosene as a cooking fuel. Rural electrification came mostly after World War II. In the area where I now live the "wire" got to some of the county by the late 1930s.

In the 1930s, Illinois was building a network of concrete roads between towns, but any improvement to most of the local roads was largely dependent on local efforts. County highway departments were established in the 1920s, I think, but the principal things done were widening, draining, grading, and keeping the road maintained between rains. They were muddy and, when frozen, very rough. During rainy seasons they were almost impassable to an automobile and even sometimes to horse-drawn vehicles.

My family's plan seems to have been to keep current cash costs under control with the sale of cream (we separated cream from the milk with a hand-cranked centrifuge) and the sale of hogs (skim milk was fed to the hogs).[3] Hogs were sold about once a year to meet interest payments on the mortgages. It seems to me that payments on the principal on the mortgage on the farm were never made.

By the time I was ready to start high school in 1925, the roads were not greatly improved in the "boondocks." Local road commissioners used large wheeled tractors to pull the road graders, but they were clumsy and slow and given to wheel spinning. Schools were tax-supported, and students were required to attend school until age sixteen. However, transportation and books were not furnished, and "snow days" were not known. Perhaps a rural school back then would close because of severe blizzard conditions, but probably this would be because the teacher could not get to the school, as for example, after a weekend. Ordinarily, lost days were made up by extending the term at year's end. In my time schools were not generally very large in numbers. The days of older people—up to age twenty or so—going to school were over. The number of classes and multiplicity of subjects taught made education something that could be a bit iffy.

During my high school days most farm kids came to school in cars or rode with someone who drove one—during good weather. When mud or snow came, we often drove one or two horses, which in an open buggy or sleigh (folding tops on the buggies) was not pleasant in rough weather. Several winters my sister, brother, and I roomed in town over the winter. This was a strain on our cash-short family finances. In my sophomore year we began to drive our Model T Ford, weather permitting. It was, I believe, the worst car I ever had anything to do with. It was also a strain on the family finances.

When I graduated from high school in 1929, most of the county roads were neither paved nor graveled, rural schools were mediocre, and the farm economy was not a cash-oriented business. Farm machinery manufacturers had begun to build row crop tractors and were building more power into smaller units. However, farmers were not buying many. They were cash-poor. One could breed a mare for about $15 (live, standing colt guaranteed), work her for most of the gestation period, and in four years have a pulling machine capable of pulling ¼ of a two-bottom plow and fueled by one's own grain and forage.

Before I leave the 1920s, I would like to point out that, in our family at least, we did not live entirely without some cultural advantages. We had several family-type magazines; they would have been considered unsophisticated today and have disappeared. We had a radio in the late '20s. We didn't have bicycles, but we were allowed to ride the six horses about. We had hand sleds and went coasting a lot in the surrounding hills. We boys built a couple of bobsleds also. Our family had some books, had library cards, and read a good deal—mostly contemporary novels, I guess, not great literature. Our family did not indulge in the general recreational practice of going to the Thursday evening summer band concerts in Mt. Carroll or even the year-round Saturday night shopping trips. Although movies were not new, I was well grown before I ever saw one. (Although your mother (Elva) grew up in a more advantaged area, her family was almost unique in its isolation, because they did not have a car until she grew up and taught school. Maybe it was snobbery, but I have always thought that both of us were really better educated than our contemporaries because of our bookish backgrounds.)

I graduated from high school in 1929. My scholarship had not been outstanding. At least two of my teachers stated that I definitely did not use my native talents. I know that I was inclined to spend little time with the subjects I disliked and to work harder on those that were more tasteful to me. My mother wanted for me to go to college, and she borrowed against an insurance policy she had to get some money. (It is likely well that she did so, because the insurance company failed during the Depression and the policyholders lost most of their premiums.) Also, because my friend John Gelwicks had a polio-crippled arm, his parents gave me a small grant to aid in his therapy. Half of my board at college was arranged for by working in the college dorm kitchen and dining room. These arrangements, together with a loan from the college for the second semester, enabled me to start at Carthage College.

Carthage was a very small (some 300 students) midwestern college. It was owned and governed by the United Lutheran Church, and ministerial students and the children of Lutheran ministers enjoyed special cost reductions. It was there in the early fall of 1929 that I met the young woman who some eleven years later became Bob's mother. (This is, however, a different story and has little bearing on the Depression, except that, as we go along, I shall likely note what effect the Depression had on our courtship and point out that we'd likely have been married some three or four years earlier if the economics of the times had been more favorable.)

During that fall the World Series of baseball was between the Chicago Cubs and the then-Philadelphia Athletics. Many of the college boys came from Chicago or that area and they were more concerned with outcome of the series than with the pending stock market crash. In fact, I doubt that one percent of the students knew what was happening. Would a financial crash of comparable magnitude be noticed with any more concern by today's eighteen- to twenty-year-olds?

These events were occurring during the thirteen years of Prohibition of the sale and manufacture of alcoholic beverages, and bootleg booze was available in most communities, but it seems to have been a minimal problem at Carthage. Possibly this was because the cost was high, and most students were of very moderate means. Recreation was limited. Athletic events were free to students and faculty. Picnics were sometimes held by various groups, and, of course, more personal pairing off and wandering about the campus was common. The village of Carthage had a movie theater with talking pictures, which were then relatively new. Some current films were shown.

The next spring's graduating class (1930) seems to have largely found placement in industry or education. At that time the State of Illinois would grant a limited teaching certificate for elementary school to those who had completed two semesters of college and had taken six credit hours of education courses. This is how I obtained my teacher's certificate. I was expected to get a job teaching and to pay my debts—perhaps down the line to earn enough to continue college later. In the spring of 1930 I got a job teaching at the Dyslin Valley School. It was a small school in a somewhat impoverished neighborhood near home. Today the site of the schoolhouse is covered by Lake Carroll. My salary was $75 per calendar month. The school term was eight months, and we were paid only for the month actually taught. That is to say, the yearly salary was $680. If my memory is correct, $5 was taken from this in each of the first three months to be paid to the Illinois Teacher's Pension Fund.

I was to stay at home and was expected to do chores in the evenings and to contribute to the family's work on weekends. The family had a pretty good Model T Ford by that time, and my brother was a senior in high school, so he used the family car. My father and I shopped around and found a seven- or eight-year-old Dodge (soft top, four door, side curtains, three-speed floorboard shift, 12-volt starter-generator, four cylinders) for $75, payable in six months by promissory note. When I think back on this, I can see that young people were unduly optimistic then too.

I was ill prepared to teach a school, even one that expected little from the teacher. The culture of the neighborhood was something of the European peasant order, mostly German. The soil was poor and did not make prosperity common. The school board was probably more interested in whether the kids liked the teacher and did not make trouble than whether they got good grades. I learned by doing—some, but not as much as was desirable. One of the director's daughters cheated on an examination. I was partly to blame as I allowed the opportunity to cheat. That was it: her father stood against rehiring me. Well, I did get hired at the next district for the same salary as before. The Depression was just beginning to be felt.

Your mother was not so fortunate. She graduated from college that spring (1931). She had majored in classical languages with enough credits in biology for a degree. Earlier graduates had been hired by industry or, that failing, had taken jobs teaching. The slots were filled. She sent out resumes to any place where there was any prospect and made some fruitless journeys to be interviewed. One place they interviewed everyone who had applied. But she came up empty. Her grades would have been almost all As, but it was a case of oversupply. That year had been very rough for her. Some of her school funds were in Orangeville's bank, which closed during the year. She also lost some small sum she had in the bank in Carthage, which also went under. I attended her graduation, and her Aunt Olive brought her folks and Aunt Edna Holt. After graduation she was obliged to go home—with a diploma and a degree and no job and very slim prospects.

Her mother had not been enthusiastic about her going to college in the beginning, and it was only with the aid and persuasion of Aunt Olive Doty that she went, at least for the last three years. Grandma Mabel did not keep her disgust (and, if it were to be truthfully told, I suspect, her disappointment) to herself. Elva's hurt was deeper probably than even I can understand. Her growing up had been, I would say, almost cloistered. The family worked hard, had little money and did not even drive a car. Some time during the years when Elva was teaching and going to college they had acquired a Model T Ford coupe, and Elva drove it, but when she wasn't there, no one did. In college she had made a few close friends and also had a few from high school days. She kept in contact with these all of her life. Otherwise, at home she withdrew into herself and, I think, formed a repugnance to the home farm—a repugnance that never really left her. I surely cannot objectively analyze some one so close to me, but I do feel that the hurt of the Depression years in her case left unhealable scars.

As I had obtained a contract with another school district, I felt quite secure. Because I was living at home and contributing my labor to the farm evenings and weekends, I was not paying board. The tires on the old Dodge were wearing out, and, of course, being young, I was wishing for new wheels. My folks must have been more tolerant than I have given them credit for. They traded the Dodge for a one-year-old Model A Ford coupe. Payments after down payment were $32.25 a month.

Since the building of the school where I went to teach that fall of '31 had burned a couple of years before, we had an almost new building. Despite that, it was rather cold, even with a basement and furnace. Also, I guess I had much to learn about firing the furnace. As it was only a couple of miles or less across the fields from home, I walked most of the time. The kids were a bit unruly. Some were not very bright, and some decidedly unwilling, but it was really a better set-up than the previous year. The schools were run by a three-man board in those days. Since one of the directors was an old man with no children in school, the other two directors ran the works. These two were cousins, and that, of course, was not so good.

By the following spring the Depression was beginning to be felt on the farms. Cash was getting scarce and some of the mortgages were in default. Consequently, school boards were looking for ways to lower taxes. You guessed it: salaries. As teachers were *looking for jobs at any price, I had to take a $30 per month cut. That wouldn't be so bad today, but it was 35 percent of my salary. It was better than nothing, which is what many were getting.*

1932 was an election year. Many people were out of work, and the politicians were glad to blame it on Hoover. Roosevelt was easily elected. He had not been in office more than a few days when he declared a "bank holiday." He issued a presidential order closing all of the banks. They could not collect debts and interest nor could they disperse funds. I am not sure how such a revolutionary action could have been constitutional, but he did it. I was issued a paycheck a few days after the election—a check where there was no place to cash it. School funds were frozen in their place of deposit. To add to this, at least one check that was issued to me came back, and I was obliged to make that up in cash. Had I been married and had a family, I would have been in deep trouble. (Dad was hardly alone as an unpaid school teacher. In 1934 Illinois was $28 million in arrears in teachers' salaries).[4]

As it was nearing tax collection time, the township treasurer was able to give teachers a partial payment of their salaries from early paid taxes. Eventually, I got all of my salary. I wonder now by what heroic measures the taxpayers were able to pay their taxes.

Back to 1933. By this time the Depression began to be perceived even by the farming community as something other and deeper than a continuation of the recession of the 1920s. That spring my teaching job went to a lower bidder. I had been receiving $55 per month. The position went to one Ruth Denner at $35 per month.[5] I was not yet twenty-two and had my Model A paid for and no money. I could drive a two- or four-horse team and operate the farm machinery of the time. I could chop down trees, split posts, cut corn by hand, etc., but those skills were in surplus. In heavy seasons labor could be had for $1 a day. Married men were taking jobs for

$15 to $20 per month and a house—maybe a pretty good house, maybe pretty bad! Extras might be negotiated, such as the meat of one hog, a quarter of beef, and wood for fuel. I stayed at home and worked for my board and lodging. Sometimes my parents squeezed out a few dollars, and an occasional day's work in busy seasons brought a few dollars for gasoline or to pay for a movie, when I went courting. First run movies with sound might be seen in Sterling for about twenty-five cents—Shirley Temple, Clark Gable, Greta Garbo, Marlene Dietrich, and Cary Grant.

In 1934, I think, mother's grandfather, C. W. Allison, who was then eighty-three or eighty-four and had lost his second wife (who had been detested and despised by her stepchildren), asked if your mother might come to cook and keep house for him in Milledgeville. Elva was glad to go. Things were not comfortable at home. The old man would pay her a pittance, and she could be more independent. He had a farm southeast of Milledgeville, which had been owned by his father, and it seems he had just paid off the mortgage on it.

By this time, farmers were either being foreclosed or their farms were turned over to the mortgager for the debt. The Mt. Carroll bank, which never reopened, held the mortgage on my parent's farm. They were unable to liquidate their debt, indeed were unable to pay the interest on it. The Federal Lank Bank set out with some government aid to take over mortgages and pay off the creditors. The Federal Lank Bank was a government-sponsored cooperative, which was organized to provide land ownership to farmers at low interest rates. Farmer committees were appointed (who were, I think, borrowers themselves) to evaluate the loans and in most cases were able to have the payments scaled down. It was a slow, tedious process, but finally my parents were able to get a scaled-down Federal Land Bank mortgage on their farm. (There is some irony in the fact that, despite Dad's hostility to Roosevelt and the

New Deal, this agency that saved his family farm was under-pinned by the Farm Credit Act of 1933, which provided funding for the Land Bank, Production Credit Associations, and the Bank of Cooperatives that in effect refinanced farm mortgages under favorable terms. These New Deal institutions, together with the Farmer's Home Administration and the Commodity Credit Corporation, became major sources of federally backed credit for farmers).[6]

I have carried this to the summer of 1934, which to most farmers in our area was perhaps the lowest point of the Depression. We had probably the driest year I have ever seen. I think this year was the beginning of the western dust bowl when the soil in the western states drifted like snow. I should say that 1936 was very hot and dry too, and for the "Okies" of the "Grapes of Wrath" was probably the height of the great drought.

In 1933 my sister Helen, who I think was a better teacher than I, was obliged to take a large cut in her salary. I think she was teaching for about $55 per month for eight months. Of course, the jobs went to the lowest bidder. Even though gas could be bought for less than twenty cents a gallon, cheap shoes for sometimes as little as $1 and overalls for about the same, there wasn't much left for luxury. My brother Homer and I delivered good hard chunk wood to the school for $12 per cord (128 cubic feet, probably about two tons). About the same time I helped old Clarence Renner thresh, and he objected because I charged him $1.50 per day. My father allowed me to cut trees and make them into posts, about six inches in diameter. They were not round, but were split out of the body wood of a burr oak tree. Abraham Lincoln would have understood that. It was similar to splitting rails, only coarser and not so long. These posts sold for fifteen cents per post.

In the fall of 1934 my first cousin Thelma Schick got the

position of teacher at Dyslin Valley School, the same place where I first taught. The nice honest guy who had given me the business when I taught there was no longer in the neighborhood. He had been obliged to sell out his farming operation to satisfy his mortgage. Thelma boarded at our house and drove her first car, a 1930 Chevrolet. Mother used the board money to buy her first power washer. Prior to that time the only concession to the mechanization of laundry at our house beyond a washboard was a lever and flywheel hand-powered washer with a crank wringer. The power washer was powered with a Briggs and Stratton air-cooled engine. It had a foot pedal starter and was a mean S.O.B. to start.

In the fall of 1935, I was offered the teaching position at the old Zion School west of Mt. Carroll, where my sister Helen had taught for two or three years. I think that because she had done a good job, they offered me the job. I got $70 per month, which was pretty good for those days. As I recall, most of the road was dirt—graded and drained pretty well, but mud when it rained, as it started to do early that fall. I drove from home every day at the beginning until winter came about Christmas. On Christmas Eve I held a Christmas program for the community, as was the custom in those days. While the program was going on, it began to snow and continued through the night. After that it got very, very cold and stayed that way until well into February. Some weeks I did not try to travel the fifteen or so miles from home to the Zion School. In fact, it would have been impossible, even with horse-drawn sleds. I boarded at the John Miller home, which was some ¾ of a mile from the school. They were hospitable people with good "Deutsch" food and warm beds (and a very cold house perched on a windy hillside).

The snow was very deep all around this area, and the winds were very strong and steady. I think if the snow had been allowed to lie still (instead of blowing into drifts), it would have covered the ground to a depth of two feet. Snow removal equipment for the most part was crude homemade plows mounted on crawler tractors, the most powerful of which was about 60 horsepower. I remember one machine operator, Billy Davis, who had built a plow on front of his "Cat" (Caterpillar) 60. I watched him one evening from the schoolhouse window. The temperature was probably about 0° and a stiff breeze was blowing. He had no cab or windbreaker of any kind on the tractor. He wore a long fur coat and high leather mittens. I suppose they probably had wool liners. As he passed, he stood up and warmed his hands on the exhaust pipe. These early plows did not remove deep drifts down to the roadbed, but had a way of rising up and leaving a hump, sometimes several feet high, in the track they made. I used to have a picture of myself standing on such a hump holding a grain scoop shovel over my head at arm's length, still unable to reach the top of the snow piled on either side of the road.

When spring came, it came rather fast, but as I remember, the red clay of the hills northwest and north of Mt. Carroll got very like the clay of which Bonnie makes ceramics. The Model A had steel spoke (wire almost) wheels, and they filled up so full with mud that they would not turn. They were almost spherical.

One last remark before we leave the winter of '36. Indoor plumbing was little known on farms.

* * * * *

Here Dad's narrative abruptly breaks off. He was unwilling to write more, but never offered an explanation. I regret now that I did not urge him more forcefully to continue. Why did he stop writing after having been so engaged in telling his story? His narrative ends shortly before he and Mother were married. Perhaps he felt that their marriage was too private to commit to paper, but my best guess is that he collided with a very painful period in his life, a time when he struggled desperately and often unsuccessfully to support his family. He was a proud man; he certainly experienced great humiliation that he didn't want to relive.

My mother and father endured extreme economic hardship in the early years of their marriage. After the wedding in February 1937 they moved to East Dubuque, Illinois, a rough Mississippi River town that had been notorious during Prohibition for bootlegging and kept its rough edges in subsequent years. Dad worked for a J. I. Case farm implement dealer, attempting to sell farm machinery and helping with repairs and spare parts. The poor farmers of northwestern Illinois and southwestern Wisconsin had little cash to buy farm equipment, however, and eventually Dad lost his job. A scant ten months after their wedding, my brother Stephen Allison Switzer was born. My father wrote a short note to his cousin Irma Jean Greve and her husband John, his heart overflowing in a rare expression of feeling: "It's a boy, born today at 11 A. M. Weighs 6 pounds 7¾ ounces. Name Stephen Allison. Everybody concerned are doing fine. I can't write further without getting sentimental and slobbery tonight. Come up and see us if you can."

My parents were ill prepared for the additional expense of a child. There were numerous subsequent moves as Dad sought employment. For a time they lived with Dad's father, Frank Switzer, on his farm near Mt. Carroll. Frank was still grieving over the death of his first wife and got along poorly with his indigent son and daughter-in-law. They moved out. They rented an abandoned schoolhouse that had been minimally converted into a family dwelling, but were evicted for failure to keep up with the rent payments. They lived for a while with Charlie and Mabel on the Orangeville farm, but again there were intergenerational frictions, so they moved to the "house behind the woods," as it came to be called in family lore, a previously abandoned house a couple of miles away. It was a wretched little house with no electricity or plumbing or heating and in a very deteriorated condition. In September 1938 my mother experienced an ectopic pregnancy, which had to be terminated surgically. The medical bills added to my parent's financial burdens. During much of this time Dad was finding work with various farmers as a day laborer, earning perhaps a dollar and a mid-day meal for a long day of hard work—when he could get it. The young family endured more than two years of extreme poverty. Dad felt the scars of it for the rest of his life.

In 1939, Stephen and Elva moved yet again, this time to Thomson, Illinois, a small sandy Mississippi River village not far from the Switzer home farm. Dad took a job in a relative's hardware store in Thomson, but that only lasted for a few months. Now, however, the economy began to improve. A huge munitions manufacturing and transshipment center, the Savanna Ordnance Depot (SOD), was built up the river outside of Savanna, which was well served by railroads and Mississippi River barges. Dad got work with the Manhattan Construction Company that built the SOD enlargement. It was a steady, relatively well-paying job. As a government contractor, the construction company hired only unionized employees. Dad attempted to join the union, only to be refused membership because he didn't have a job in construction—a perfect no-win situation. Eventually the union relented, but this experience and the behavior of the union stewards in bestowing obvious favoritism and encouraging featherbedding engendered an enduring hostility toward labor unions in my prickly and proud father. It was hard, dirty, unskilled labor, but Dad was very strong and very willing, and glad to earn a decent wage for the first time in years.

When the construction phase was finished, Dad didn't want to follow the construction company to a new site, so he got work at SOD itself, loading and storing munitions. During this time I was born, in August 1940. Our family had settled in a very modest little rented house in Thomson that had no indoor plumbing or central heat, though it did boast electricity and a telephone. There was a barn in back where Dad kept two cows for milk, selling the excess. Mother made butter and cottage cheese, and Dad used the cows' manure to fertilize a family garden. The old Model A Ford was traded for a used 1937 Pontiac. Because my Dad's family was well known in Thomson, our family had a ready circle of relatives and friends. In 1943 my brother started elementary school in Thomson. In spite of the horrible war raging in Europe and in the Pacific, Stephen and Elva's little family seemed to be emerging from their misery.

However, World War II eventually reached deeply into their lives when Dad was drafted in early 1944. Although he was almost thirty-three years old, worked in a munitions plant, and had a wife and two little boys to support, the demands of the war effort forced the local draft board to take many men with families. Dad elected to serve in the Navy and, after stateside training, was shipped to the South Pacific. Although he hated the waste and disruption of the war, his military experiences took him to fascinating parts of the world, and his subsequent years were sprinkled with stories from his time in the service. The war ended abruptly in August of 1945, but demobilization of the great armies and navies took time; Dad did not arrive home in Thomson until the early spring of 1946.

During that spring an important family drama was played out, although I only became aware of it years later. After the war my father was almost thirty-five years old, but he had yet to get a start in life. He had no education beyond a year in college. He had not established a line of work before the war. He could not return to his job making munitions at the Savanna Ordnance Deport. Above all, he had acquired a hearty dislike of working under the supervision of others. Growing up on a farm in Carroll County was the normal preparation for a life of farming, and he wanted to operate his own farm. Moreover, both his widowed father and my mother's parents were keen to retire. Both sets of parents urged my father to take over their farms. The decision turned on practical grounds. Both farms were quite backward—no indoor plumbing or central heat, no modern farm machinery. The Switzer farm didn't even have electrical service. My paternal grandfather's farm was larger, but lay on much poorer land. Furthermore, Dad had two siblings whose shares would eventually have to be bought. My mother was an only child and would inherit the farm outright. To add to the pressure, my mother's parents threatened to sell the farm if my parents did not take it over. My mother did not want to return to farming, particularly not to the primitive farm where she had grown up. She knew it was a brutally hard life, that the summers were hot and the winters cold, and that dairy cows never take a holiday. Her mother had worked like a man, as her father said, but my mother was small, frail, and often unwell. She had grown used to the relative comforts of small town life. She had a college degree and a teacher's certificate. She could have taken a job as a teacher, but she felt—as women of her generation generally did—that she belonged in the home with her young boys. My father's will was strong and he belonged to a time and family in which husbands ruled their families. They (or rather he) decided to move to my mother's parents' farm, the Charlie Allison farm near Orangeville.

My parents lived there until they died. But it was a decision that my mother never accepted in her heart, one that diminished her life. I think that my father knew this and resented it, and I know that they both paid a sad, enervating price for it. I never heard them dispute this life-altering decision openly, but I felt the consequences of the subsurface disagreement throughout the rest of their lives.

The Switzer farm in 1977.

Chapter Three

Stephen and Elva Modernize the Farm (1946–1957)

When our family moved from Thomson to my grandparent's farm in the summer of 1946, we were in many ways stepping back into farm life of the early twentieth century. Charlie and Mabel owned no modern machinery and operated only horse-powered equipment. Their style of agriculture had changed only modestly since 1916. The farmhouse had no indoor toilets, no central heat, and no running water. An outdoor outhouse served the family's sanitary needs all year around. All cooking was still done on a kitchen range. My parents had grown up on farms under similar conditions, so it was hardly a shock to return to them, but the success of their farm and their physical comfort required strenuous and expensive modernization.

Charlie and Mabel had made a few changes during the late 1930s and early '40s. They now hired neighboring farmers to bale hay and straw (The baling wire and twine provided Charlie with raw material for dozens of improvised uses and repairs. It was a family joke that everything was held together with "hay wire.") The grain was now harvested by hiring a farmer to combine it. A mobile tractor-drawn threshing machine with a cutter-feeder mouth cut the standing dry grain, threshed it, and separated the grain from the straw as it moved through the field. The term "combine" came from the fact that cutting and threshing were combined in a single operation. These machines speeded the harvest and reduced the labor required, but added the cost of cash payments for the hired machinery and operator.

The biggest change introduced by Charlie and Mabel was electrification of the farm in the late 1930s or early 1940s. The house and barn now had electrical lighting. Mabel used an electric iron, occasionally a hot plate, and an electrically powered (but still labor-intensive) washing machine. Water from the well was pumped with an electric motor rather than relying on the windmill, a balky single-cylinder McCormick-Deering gasoline engine, or pumping by hand. The chore of milking the cows was made faster and easier by use of a milking machine, which was activated by an electrically powered vacuum pump, but this was not installed until 1944.

A simple party line telephone system had been added to the farm by 1946.[1] The same circuit connected several farms. Anyone on the party line could be reached by ringing his code by turning a hand-cranked magneto built into the telephone, which hung on the wall. Our code was three long rings. We all knew the codes for our neighbors, so we knew when and who received a call. There was nothing to prevent eavesdropping on the party line, and it was a popular form of rural entertainment. If we wanted to call someone outside of the party line, we cranked the operator's code (one long ring), and she made the necessary connections from her switchboard in Orangeville. One very long uninterrupted ring was a community emergency signal and was used to summon help for a fire. This old-fashioned system continued to be used on our farm until the late 1950s. The telephone simplified grocery shopping for Mabel. Now she could ring "central" to telephone the "egg man," the grocer who bought her farm eggs for his store, and give him a list of items to bring when he collected eggs at the farm.

In the immediate postwar period it was difficult to buy new farm tractors or machinery, because all the manufacturing facilities had been converted to war production.[2] Dad knew he had to convert to tractor-powered agriculture, but was not able to buy a tractor until 1947 or 1948.[3] Then he bought a rather old Case Model CC tractor, which could only be started by hand-cranking. So, for the first couple of years we farmed with horses, as Grandpa and Grandma Allison had done. Grandpa had a pair of geldings, Prince and Barney. Dad added a mare named Rosie from his father's farm. These were large, broad, strong, but slow draft horses, not the sleek animals favored by horse lovers today. Prince and Barney were mean and only minimally willing, but Rosie was a gentle horse, who had been broken to ride. My brother and I occasionally rode her bareback on a Sunday afternoon for recreation. Dad hired a tractor for spring plowing, as well as hiring hay baling and combining, but all of the other fieldwork was done with the horses. Even after the old Case tractor was purchased and a newer Case Model DC was added around 1950, we used the horses for many jobs. My brother and I both learned to put harnesses on the horses and to drive the team, even though we were still quite small. The horses were finally sold in the 1950s, first the two geldings, then dear old Rosie. Dad discreetly arranged to have her trucked away while we were both in school. Whether she was destined for slaughter, like loyal old Boxer in *Animal Farm*, I never knew.

In the early 1940s Charlie and Mabel were offered the chance to sell a large amount of limestone gravel for use in converting area roads from dirt to gravel-paved roads. The gravel was dug out of a steep hillside in a field southwest of the farm buildings. My grandparents badly needed the money, but they disliked the noise, dust, and occasional blasting as big trucks hauled stone to be crushed on the site and then out to the roadbeds. An ugly yellow-gray gravel pit scarred the hillside, which Grandpa bitterly regretted. By 1946 the gravel pit was no longer active, but it served Grandpa and Dad as a place to dump all sorts of worn-out machinery, old wire fencing, used lumber, remnants of uprooted trees, even disused small buildings. For my brother and me and our friends, the gravel pit was a wonderful site for play. We scoured its walls and stone heaps for fossils and colorful rocks. We romped all over it, playing fantasy games. The pit resembled the southwestern desert scenery favored by cowboy and Indian movies of the time, a resemblance that fueled our imagination. Over the years the great scar has been healed substantially by erosion, natural growth of grasses, and by several modifications of its roughest areas by bulldozer, as Dad sought to make it less of an eyesore and to reclaim some pasture from it.

A major source of support for Dad's efforts to move the farm toward more modern agriculture came from a special education program for World War II veterans who had begun farming. Like all vets, Dad was eligible for support for higher education from the G.I. Bill, but it was obviously impossible for him to both operate a farm and go to college. The Veteran's Administration set up the On-Farm Training program for veterans like Dad to take classes in modern agricultural science, which were taught by the local high school vocational agriculture (vo-ag) teachers in Orangeville, Roy Hefty and Boyd Henry, in the evenings.[4] The instructors also made many on-farm visits for inspections and further instruction. Veterans in the program received monthly subsistence payments in place of college expenses, which were a boon to our cash-poor family. By 1954, nearly one million veterans had received training under the On-Farm program.

The vo-ag teachers helped the veteran farmers to adopt new methods emerging from research. Dad learned to classify his fields according to their optimal crop uses. He tested the soils for acidity and nutrient deficiencies, which could be corrected by commercial fertilizers. A dramatic example was the introduction of alfalfa as the major hay and pasture crop. This hardy legume produces hay of much higher nutrient value than the grass-clover mixtures Charlie grew. Moreover, the plant forms a symbiotic relationship with root-dwelling rhizobia, bacteria that fix organic nitrogen for the plant from nitrogen gas in the air and greatly enrich the soil for subsequent crops. Charlie knew this, but maintained that his attempts to grow alfalfa had failed. Soil testing demonstrated that the land was too acidic for good alfalfa growth. An application of powdered limestone corrected the problem, and we soon grew luxuriant crops of alfalfa. Dad also bought inocula of the appropriate *Rhizobium* strain and mixed it with his alfalfa seed prior to planting to ensure an optimal infection of the roots with the friendly bugs. Dad adopted the use of commercial hybrid seed and, later, commercial fertilizer, herbicides and pesticides, which greatly increased his yields per acre, especially of corn. Dad's father, Frank Switzer, became a DeKalb seed dealer when he retired from farming and strongly encouraged him to adopt hybrid seed.

In the rolling hills of northwestern Illinois, water erosion of plowed fields was a serious problem made worse by the common practice of plowing in straight rows up and down the hills, creating ready-made ditches. Grandpa Charlie's fields were scarred by a number of ditches, some with willow trees growing in them, most impassible by machinery. The vo-ag teachers encouraged the farmers to plow and plant their fields on the contour. The direction of plowing was altered to follow approximately level paths and curve gently around the hills. The lower lying valleys where the water collected and flowed downhill were always left in grass and were never plowed. Contour farming greatly reduces soil erosion and conserves water during dry periods. An ardent conservationist, Dad adopted the practice enthusiastically. His conservative and opinionated father growled, "By Gol', Steve, the sun has warped your corn rows!" Dad also constructed a series of dirt terraces by plowing the soil into high ridges that followed the contour lines in the fields north of the farm buildings. The terraces retained water from snowmelt and heavy spring rains and directed the excess to waterways well away from the buildings. This simple measure ended Charlie and Mabel's annual muddy flooding of the barnyard.

Dad made changes in our animal husbandry as well. The unprofitable chicken flock was discontinued, and the raising of hogs began. At first, we had only a few sows, which had the run of the barnyard. One big gentle sow permitted us boys to ride her like a pony, accepting scratching behind her ears as a reward. She had a flock of piglets, which followed her around squealing and nagging until she abruptly flopped down on her side and allowed the little row of piggies to nurse greedily. When the size of the herd increased, the swine were confined to fields and hog houses and only one other pig was made into a pet. Dad used the McLean County system of hog sanitation.[5] That is, he moved the hogs to new ladino clover/alfalfa pastures every year to reduce their exposure to infectious disease, and to enrich their diet with the nitrogen-rich legumes. Swine culture was labor-intensive. Daily hauling of water, whey, and ground feed were required. None of this was automated, as is nearly universal today. We also had to catch the young weanling pigs to put rings in their noses (to pre-vent them from rooting up the ladino-alfalfa sod on which they were raised) and to castrate the males—both very unpleasant tasks. Vaccination against swine cholera and erysipelas was later added. During the cold early spring days when the new litters were born, we kept a sharp eye for a sow about to give birth so she could be safely confined in her own pen. As boys with smaller hands, my brother or I were occasionally called on, frequently in the middle of the night, to serve as a midwife for a young sow who was having difficulty with delivery. (We all took part in midwife-ry with young cows now and then, a very dramatic operation in-volving ropes and pulleys—surprisingly, usually completely successful for mother and calf.)

In the 1940s and early 1950s, Dad kept a bull, as Charlie had done, so that the cows could be bred and bear a calf annually. The bull was kept in a stout wooden stall in the barn and only allowed out to perform his reproductive duties, which he did quickly and brutally. Sex had little mystery for my brother and me, even when we were quite young. We were taught to observe the signs of a cow in heat ("bullin'," we called it), so she could be mated. The bull had an aluminum ring in his nose; a long pipe-like staff with a latch in the end was linked to the ring to lead the huge beast out for watering or cleaning his stall. The bulls were large, dangerous animals; a mature bull could weigh more than 2,000 pounds. On a couple of occasions our bull twisted his way free from Dad and ran out into the fields. Dad mounted Rosie and chased him down, while my brother and I watched from a safe refuge.

The introduction of "the bull who drives a car"—artificial insemination of our cows by a technician who used the semen from very fine, genetically screened bulls—brought a big improve-ment to the dairy herd. The danger of the bull was eliminated, but, more importantly, the improved genetics gave us female calves that would grow up to produce more and richer milk. According to a study by the USDA, artificial insemination was responsible for a 57 percent increase in the amount of milk produced per cow and a 54 percent increase in the butterfat content of the milk from 1924 to 1954.[6] Dad was late in adopting the new technology, but his dairy herd eventually showed similar gains in productivity. In the years from 1952 to 1955, when my brother and I were studying agriculture at Orangeville High School, Dad introduced the practice of monthly weighing and sampling of the milk from each cow. We performed the Babcock butterfat analysis in a little lab at the high school. The records allowed us to calculate an approximate annual milk and butterfat production from each cow. This gave Dad a much more rational basis for culling less productive cows from the herd and for deciding which calves to save for his future cows. The daughters of productive cows were much more likely to be high milk producers, especially if their sire by artificial insemination was a bull with a proven record of transmitting high productivity to his daughters. After we boys left high school Dad continued the testing, using a commercial lab.

Dad was not the only farmer to adopt these new methods of agriculture, of course. Nearly all American farmers did. The consequence of modern mechanization, hybrid seed, extensive use of chemical fertilizer and pesticides, improved animal genetics, and vaccination resulted in large increases in productivity in the late 1940s and throughout the next decade and beyond. Farm production outran demand, and the consequent surpluses suppressed the prices farmers received throughout the period.[7] From 1945 to 1950 the average prices of agricultural products rose by an average of about five percent per year, but from 1951 to 1956 they fell 23 percent.[8] The federal government struggled to deal with the farm surpluses and to prop up farm prices with various programs. Since my parents did not sell wheat, corn, or bulk milk off the farm, these price support and acreage set-aside programs only indirectly affected their receipts. In fact, Dad argued that they placed an effective cap at a low level on farm prices, and he decried the waste, which was symbolized by the fields of round steel corn-cribs filled with surplus corn that dotted the countryside for years. While conditions were certainly not as bad as during the 1920s and '30s, farm prices were relatively flat throughout the 1950s and '60s, while prices farmers paid for machinery and supplies rose steadily.[9]

Farmers raise their animals humanely, but as the animals are eventually destined for the slaughterhouse, they generally do not become household pets. Our tenderhearted mother made an exception in the case of Polly the Pig. She was also fond of the semi-feral barn cats that are found on dairy farms, and she and we boys made pets of most of them. Burt Cramer, an occasional hired man, shot and wounded a pigeon that blundered into our barnyard. The bird had a metal band on his leg and was less frightened of humans than normal, so we deduced that it was a domesticated bird. Since it was no longer capable of flight, Mother nursed it back to health and gave it a home in a cardboard box in our kitchen. Dubbed J. Wellington Coo after a Chinese ambassador to the United States, the pigeon became a surprisingly companionable and intelligent pet. It stomped and cooed in its little house when agitated, but otherwise followed Mother faithfully around the house and garden.

But Polly the Pig broke the rule against having genuine farm animals as pets. As a newly born piglet she became separated from her mother and was rejected by her. Dad brought the chilled and shivering little pink creature to the house, where Mother wrapped it in warm blankets and fed it bits of warm cow's milk with an eyedropper and later a spoon. Most attempts to rescue such abandoned piglets fail, but Polly survived, and within a few days she was fully healthy and grew rapidly. She outgrew her home in the kitchen and was moved to the adjacent washhouse/summer kitchen, still later to a pen in the unused chicken house. She was affectionate and extremely intelligent, grunting happily when scratched and pressing her wet nose to our shoes. Eventually, she became a nuisance; she preferred the house to being outside, learned to open doors, and peeked through cracks in the barn door to learn when the coast was clear for her to run in and plunge her greedy head into a bucket of warm fresh milk. Had Polly been a male, she would have been destined for the castrating knife (becoming a "barrow") and sold for pork at six months of age. Since she was a "gilt" (a female pig that has not yet borne a litter), Polly eventually joined our herd of brood sows. We always said that "she thinks she's people," though, and she never fully integrated into the herd. She sometimes escaped her pen and sought human companionship. Polly wasn't much better as a mother sow than her own mother had been, so she eventually had to be sold for slaughter, an event my mother mourned privately.

As we moved into the 1950s, Dad continued to buy more modern machinery. However, he was always cash-poor and debt-averse, so he tended to buy used equipment at farm auctions. This was not always a wise choice. The old equipment was subject to frequent breakdowns. Much valuable harvest time was lost while Dad made trips to implement dealers for replacement parts and worked on the repairs, which he did himself, if at all possible. Eventually he bought his own hay baler and grain combine, because he was so frustrated with waiting until hired machinery came to harvest overripe and storm-damaged crops.

An old Model A Ford pickup truck was purchased in the late 1940s, followed by a couple of Chevrolet flatbed trucks. The first of the Chevys had a troublesome tendency to break axles, perhaps aggravated by my brother's energetic driving. My brother and I learned to drive these trucks and the farm tractors when we were still quite young. At first, I found the heavy, stiff controls too difficult to operate, and I wasn't strong enough to crank the old Case. But my brother was doing these things, and I wanted to be a big boy too. By the age of ten or eleven, I was strong enough to start driving tractors. My brother loved the old Model A truck and quickly learned to drive it. He and Dad taught me to drive it too when I was about twelve. At first we drove the truck only around the farm, but before long, we were driving it to deliver milk to the cheese factory a mile away or for other chores on local roads. Like most farm boys, we were driving trucks and cars illegally on country roads years before we were old enough (fifteen, later sixteen) to obtain a driving license. Of course, our ability to drive tractors and operate farm machinery was important to getting the fieldwork done, and we were active operators from the age of twelve or thirteen on.

For the first few years that we lived on the farm the improvements to our house and the quality of domestic life did not keep pace with agricultural modernization. The old farmhouse was cold and drafty in the winter. Only the kitchen and living room were islands of warmth. I recall suffering from chilblains during those early years. This is a condition in which chronically cold toes become swollen and red and very itchy when they finally warm up. My parents replaced the old pot-bellied coal-burning stove with little isinglass windows in the living room with an oil-burning space heater equipped with an electric blower. This improved the heating of the downstairs, but the upstairs rooms where my brother and I slept were unheated. We were warm enough under many layers of blankets and quilts, but undressing at night and getting up on frosty mornings were damned cold. We grabbed our clothes and ran downstairs to sit in front of the oil burner fan while we dressed. We were allowed to use chamber pots for the night's urine, but during the day, a frigid trip to the outdoor outhouse was required.

Mother did all of the cooking and heating of water for laundry and once-weekly baths on the kitchen range. Mondays brought the all-day laundry chores for her. Even though we used an electric washing machine, water was carried by hand, heated on the range, dumped into the washer and rinse tubs, and emptied by hand. Wet clothing was fed through a wringer by hand, rinsed and wrung again, then hung on outside lines—summer and winter alike.

The cold, drafty house was bad for Mother's health. During the 1940s she suffered from bad colds and pneumonia repeatedly and required hospitalization several times. Once, I recall my surprise and embarrassment at seeing Dad kiss Mother when we left her bedside after a visit to the hospital. I had never seen my parents express affection physically before. Then there was the matter of Dad's cooking during Mother's absences. He was a dreadful cook, and his pancakes became a family legend. His first attempts were paper-thin and burned. He overcorrected in preparing the second batch; these pancakes were very thick and full of uncooked dough. We gave them to the farm dog, Vicky, who was notorious for eating all manner of disgusting things—a cow's afterbirth, for example. Vicki took Dad's pancakes to the garden and buried them! Dad and Mom began a campaign to modernize the house. Since Charlie and Mabel still owned the farm and were renting to my parents "on the shares" (also called "on the halves"), they had to pay for major improvements to the buildings. Charlie, and especially Mabel, were reluctant to cover the costs of modernizing the house. The dispute was kept largely out of view of my brother and me, but I understand that my parents eventually threatened to leave the farm if improvements were not made.

The first project agreed on was indoor plumbing. Perhaps because the farm's well water was very hard, they decided to dig a concrete-lined cistern behind the house. Mabel complained that nine hundred dollars was a lot to pay for "a hole in the ground." Gutters were attached to the eaves of the roof, and rainwater was collected in the cistern. The soft rainwater was pumped into the summer kitchen and the main kitchen. An indoor toilet was not installed at that time. The decision to supply the house with rainwater turned out to be a bad one. The new cistern leaked, and the contractor's half-hearted efforts to repair the leaks never succeeded. Worse, leaves from the many trees surrounding the house collected in the gutters, clogging them and the downspouts. Leaves washed into the cistern; the collected water was stained an amber color. The water was not fit for drinking or cooking, so water for those uses was still carried from the well.

Our family got by with the crude rainwater system for a couple of years, but by 1950 my parents' dissatisfaction boiled over again, and a much more complete modernization was undertaken in 1951. The cistern was abandoned, and the plumbing was connected to fresh water from the well located under the old windmill. A bathroom was installed in a little bedroom that lay just off of the living room. A cesspool was dug and the sinks, new flush toilet, and bathtub were connected to it. The drainpipe from the house to the cesspool was improperly laid, however, so that it tended to plug up and flood the basement with sewage. This was most likely to happen when we had company, who used the toilet and toilet paper more lavishly than our family had learned to do, much to Mother's annoyance. Dad had the hard, nasty job of clearing the drain line with a long flexible cable. Until the 1970s, Mother continued to drain her laundry water by a hose out onto the ground for fear of plugging the sewer line. Still, the bathroom was attractive and comfortable. A large storage closet was built at one end of the room. It was a big improvement over the outhouse and the once weekly baths in a big galvanized tub in the kitchen. (By 1952, my brother and I were taking showers after gym classes every day at Orangeville High School and only used the bathtub during the summer.)

An equally important improvement in 1951 was the installation of an oil-fired furnace in the basement and central heating. Perhaps the term "central heating" exaggerates the system a bit. The downstairs rooms were adequately heated, although we continued to use the coal/wood kitchen range for both cooking and heating until the 1970s. Vents to the front parlor were closed, and its doors were kept shut in winter. Vents served the five upstairs rooms, but the system was not designed to do more than take the chill off the air on cold days. You could see your breath in little white clouds in the winter. Some insulation was placed in the attic, but the walls were not insulated, and the house's many large windows were drafty, even with storm windows installed. The major improvements to the house were completed by 1952. No further big changes were made until the entire old kitchen/wash house was torn down and replaced by a new kitchen and laundry room two decades later—only five years before Mother died.

After the modernization, Mother set about redecorating the house. She eventually repainted the walls and replaced the wallpaper in all but two smaller upstairs rooms used only for storage, which were left in their original condition. The ancient woodwork and wainscotting had been painted many, many times. Completely stripping the paint was too arduous. Mother had to be content with removing the loose paint and painting over. She hired a local lady to hang the wallpaper and chose figured floral patterns. (She permitted my brother and me to select the wallpaper for our bedrooms, so we picked more masculine patterns. Mine featured books, boy's hobby items, and lab equipment.) The wood plank floors in the house were painted, but worn and extremely uneven because the foundation had settled in various directions. My parents installed vinyl tile over the kitchen and living room floors, which gave them a more modern appearance and was easier to clean. However, the tiles frequently came loose and gave us ongoing maintenance problems. By the mid-1950s the "modernization" of the farmhouse was essentially complete. It certainly had not been lavishly done. In fact, my parents were always concerned about minimizing costs. Little more was done until the kitchen was finally replaced in 1972, and Dad later removed unused and leaking chimneys, replaced the roofing, and repainted the deteriorating house in the 1980s.

* * * * *

Although our parents modernized our farming methods and improved the buildings, the overall character of our farm was little changed from Charlie and Mabel's practices. We raised the same crops: corn, oats, and hay or pasture in rotation. The farm was a dairy farm on which large numbers of hogs were also raised. Our farm was quite typical of the farms in our area.

As a family farm, it was typical in another way: its operation was very dependent on unpaid family labor, including child labor. Farm children are explicitly exempted from child labor laws. Dad assigned chores to my brother and to me as soon as he took over the farm. This was normal practice for the time, and I assume that it still is: everyone contributes his share to a farm family's work-load.[10] At first, the chores were fairly light tasks, such as gathering eggs and feeding chickens or scattering bedding in the cattle stalls. As we grew bigger and stronger, the jobs became more numerous and strenuous. My brother was almost three years older, so he got the heavier work first, but our chores were similar by the time I was twelve. We were required to get up every morning by six or six-thirty for chores, which included helping with milking, carry-ing and filtering the milk, feeding grain and hay to the cows, and carrying feed and water for the hogs. We worked for an hour or two before washing up, eating breakfast, changing clothes, and then hurrying off to school.

Neither of us was a very willing chore boy—especially in the mornings, least of all on winter mornings. Mother often had to call up the steep stairs many times to get us out of our warm beds. Now and then, Dad grew impatient with our stalling and stormed upstairs in his barn clothes, angrily driving us out of our beds. After school, around four in the afternoon, we changed back into our chore clothes and repeated the morning's jobs. Many other chores were added on weekends and holidays: cleaning the ma-nure out of the barn and hog houses; washing the milking ma-chine parts, milk pails, and strainers (an especially miserable job in winter because there was no milk house and hot water had to be carried from the house); shoveling grain for grinding feed; and on and on.

During the summer months when school was not in ses-sion, the farm's fieldwork filled our days. As soon as we were strong enough to manipulate the tractors' controls, we boys oper-ated them for essentially all of the farming operations. Dad did most of the spring plowing and corn picking because these were done when we were in school, but there was little else we had not mastered by our early teens. Operating the machinery required some skill and coordination. Other chores were simply heavy work: lifting ten-gallon milk cans full of milk, loading and storing bales of hay, shoveling corn and oats or manure. Brother Steve and I grew tall, lean, and strong, although we never developed Dad's massive musculature. I preferred the fieldwork to any other because I suffered less from hot weather than from the cold, and I liked the sense of visible accomplishment as a field was fully harvested or great mounds of grain accumulated. We worked every day on the morning and evening barn chores, but we generally did not work in the fields on Sundays. Ours was not a religious family (a rarity in our community, but there were surprisingly few attempts to evangelize our family), but Dad respected his neighbor's sensibilities about working on the Sabbath. We boys welcomed the partial holiday.

Although my brother and I were not particularly enthusiastic farm workers—indeed, we were at times downright balky—we knew how to do our jobs well. As we became teenagers, we were both stronger and more capable as well as more rebellious. Some of this was the inevitable straining of adolescent youth for independence, and a natural dislike of hard physical labor. However, Dad's managerial style contributed to the strain. He gave orders and he didn't accept opposition. He didn't make us partners in decisions or invite our ideas about how a problem might be solved. He was quick to anger over a job undone or done incorrectly, but he was stingy with praise or expressions of satisfaction or gratitude for a job well done. Balking at this was counterproductive, of course, but I was at times a sulky worker. I can recall only one time when we were whipped with a willow switch for stalling too long on chores, but Dad's authority was absolute even without physical punishment. In this, he was probably a typical farm father—and he was considerably less harsh than his own father had been. Yet he failed to make either Steve or me feel as though we were partners in a shared, mutually beneficial enterprise. Little wonder that both of us left home as soon as we finished high school.

Mother, on the other hand, had Grandpa Charlie's knack for making work done for her feel appreciated and collegial. When planting and weeding her garden or harvesting and canning fruits and vegetables became too much for her to do alone, she persuaded Dad to release me from fieldwork to help her. The work was lighter, of course, and she was so appreciative that I welcomed these assignments. That she usually asked for me to help her reflected a favoritism that I suspect became hurtful to my brother and to Dad. She and I were more temperamentally alike; we had both excelled in and loved schoolwork. It was natural that our relationship would develop a special closeness, but it had some unfortunate effects on the cohesiveness of our family.

Of course, we boys did have some free time, and the farm offered great open spaces for outdoor play. In 1949 or 1950 we acquired bicycles and rode them around the neighborhood. Two or three nearby farms had children our age whom we already knew well from school. These kids were our favorite companions during our infrequent summer days off. Our friends and their families exposed us to a bit of the world, with different views and experiences—valuable for kids living in such isolated circumstances. Not least of our discoveries were insights—not always accurate—into the mysteries of human sexuality. From one family in particular I absorbed the sense that the coming of sexual maturity was an event to be happily anticipated, that fun and physical pleasure were to be expected—not a lesson I had heard at home.

I was also quite content with solitary recreation. I set up a combination workshop-lab, first in a small, unused outbuilding, later in the basement of the house. After the furnace was installed, the basement lab was available year-round. I was fond of building model vehicles and airplanes, but my favorite activities focused on science and nature. I collected birds' eggs and nests from around the farm. When the old oil burner was removed from our living room, we discovered a perfectly preserved little skeleton of a mouse under it. I carefully glued the bones back into their proper locations and mounted the skeleton on a polished wooden base. This stimulated a collection of skeletons of small animals, which my friends thought was a bit bizarre, but taught me a lot about anatomy. I collected various supplies for a chemistry laboratory from commercially available chemistry sets and other sources, and was fond of performing experiments. For the most part, I had no clear understanding of what I was doing until I began to study science in high school. No matter; my curiosity was stimulated, and I dreamed of becoming a scientist. Today, I maintain that it is not essential that a child's involvement with science be didactically rigorous—it is enough to fascinate and to puzzle. Often I understood only years later the reasons for the observations I made in my childhood lab.

From September through May, my brother and I were in school. Beginning in 1946, we attended Pleasant Hill School—the same one-room school on the corner of our farm that our mother had attended from 1916 to 1921. The building was a little changed from Mother's day. It had been raised by about four feet, and a basement was excavated under it. A coal-burning hot air furnace was installed in the basement, which also provided a play area during bad weather. When the building was wired for electricity its large, drafty west windows, previously needed to illuminate the classroom, were boarded over. Otherwise, little had been changed. The children sat in wooden desks of various sizes in one large room with an elevated stage in the front. We used outdoor toilets until around 1949, when chemical toilets were installed in the former boys' and girls' cloakrooms. Pulling a rope rang a bell in a cupola on the roof to summon the children at the start of day and from the twice-daily recesses. One teacher taught all subjects to all eight grades—if there were children attending at each grade level. Enrollment was usually fifteen to twenty pupils. All were farm children. Before 1951 my brother and I only took baths once a week in a big galvanized tub with water heated on the kitchen range. We used the same water and entertained ourselves by listening to the radio on Sunday afternoon. Given that we worked in the barn morning and night, we must have been a bit aromatic when we went to school, in spite of changing into clean school overalls. I remember often having rather scaly, discolored skin at the wrists because of the constant rubbing of wet barn clothes. All of the school kids must have been similarly grubby, because I don't recall anyone being teased for it.

This kind of rural education has disappeared from America, except in a few very sparsely settled western states, and is considered quite inadequate today. In my experience, however, it was surprisingly effective. With the exception of one inept and immature young woman who taught the year I was in fifth grade, our teachers provided a good basic education in all subjects at all levels to children with a broad range of abilities. There was no formal education in science, art, music, foreign languages, or physical education, which must be seen as deficiencies. But reading, spelling, and writing, arithmetic to simple algebra, English literature and grammar, geography and history were well taught. I *loved* school. I loved it not only because it provided all-day relief from the drudgery of farm chores, but also because it was easy and interesting (well, not long division, but most of it). A bright student could complete his deskwork quickly and then explore the school's book collection or listen to the more advanced classes recite during their sessions in front of the teacher's desk. The school's books, while often out-of-date (our encyclopedia only referred to "the World War"), were suitable for all eight grade levels. A self-paced reader could move readily to more advanced material. The year I was to be in second grade, there were no other second grade pupils. When the teacher discovered that I had no difficulty doing the same work as the two third graders, I skipped the second grade altogether. My parents gave their permission for this, but the county superintendent of schools had refused it, so I have always joked that it was illegal. A result was that I was always a year younger than my classmates and graduated from high school at age sixteen.

As the years passed and a favorite friend, Eddie Barker, moved away, I found myself wishing for more friends of my own age. My brother completed eighth grade in 1951 and started riding a yellow school bus to the high school in Orangeville. He dropped his childhood name of "Allison" and began using his first name, Steve. He acquired a new circle of friends and quickly became involved in more adult activities. In 1952 a new building, in which the junior high school (seventh and eighth grades) and the high school were combined, opened in Orangeville. As I started eighth grade that fall, I joined my brother on the daily bus ride into the village and entered the more grown-up, less innocent world of high school. This was a period of rapid consolidation of one-room schools in Illinois. In 1945 there were 9,680 such one-room school districts; following a 1947 law that provided for the creation of community unit distracts, the number of one-room school districts dwindled to 906 by 1957, but the number of one-room schools actually in use was already down to 722 in 1954.[11] In 1953, all of the Orangeville's one-room country grade schools were closed, and the school children were bused to consolidated schools in the village. A rustic era of rural education had passed.

Our high school years ultimately had a big impact on the future of our family farm, because they reinforced for both my brother and myself the desire for a life away from it. For my brother this future was ill-defined at the time, but he grew to yearn for independence and autonomy. Like most teenagers, he loved automobiles. For a rural teenager especially, an automobile equals freedom. It opens the door to after-school sports events and social activities. A car was the only way from the farm to the high school after class hours. You drove your own car, begged a ride from a friend who had one, or used the family car—if permission could be gotten. Having your own car was the passport to freedom: freedom to cruise the village streets and rural roads at night, to pursue innocent entertainment and not-so-innocent amusements. Steve bought an old 1941 Ford and joined this exciting adolescent world. Before long, his adventures brought him into conflict with our parents. He was out too late too often, and needed money for gas. Not all of his friends or nighttime activities met with my parents' approval. His grades suffered. His frequent conflicts with Dad during these years, while a normal part of adolescence, solidified his desire for an independent life away from the farm. If they ever discussed the idea of farming as partners, I never heard of it. Dad would have been very limited in what he could offer in any case, because he and Mother did not buy the farm from Grandpa Charlie until 1959, long after Steve had struck out on his own.

I was less openly rebellious, and I was too young to get a driver's license until I was a senior in high school, but my determination to leave the farm was intensified by my high school education in science. I had expected to love biology and I did, but high school chemistry changed my view of science forever. The course was taught by Wallace Graves, a rather rigid and demanding but highly intelligent teacher. Graves presented chemistry at a level more suitable for college freshmen; he was completely unwilling to pitch his course to the average student. (As a result, the Orangeville district did not renew his contract the following year.) I was delighted with the structure, order, and rigor with which chemistry illuminated the nature of matter. Some of Graves's demonstrations of organic chemistry provided the insight that natural products—the stuff of which living cells are made—were chemicals too, subject to the same beautiful underlying chemical science as nonliving matter. I sought a combination between biology and chemistry and decided that it must be biochemistry, even though I had only a vague idea as to what that discipline was. Encouraged by my mother, I formed a fierce determination to study chemistry in college, to go to graduate school and earn a Ph.D. in biochemistry, and become a researcher or college professor. I yearned for it. I daydreamed about it. I planned my entire high school program to prepare for college admission requirements—as best I could in a small rural high school.

There were less noble motivations too. Like my brother, I wanted to escape my father's domination and the tyranny of chores and farm labor. College would be my "wings," I repeated to myself, my escape to a happier, easier, more satisfying and more autonomous life. I was both running toward a dream and running away from home.

With my parents in front of the farmhouse in 1966.

Chapter Four

The Boys Leave Home: Stephen and Elva Alone (1957–1977)

Beginning in the 1950s and throughout the 1970s, the pace of farm consolidation increased. The total number of U.S. farms declined from 5.4 million in 1950 to 2.3 million in 1978; there was a corresponding increase in average farm acreage from 216 to 449 acres.[1] A typical pattern was for a successful farmer who already owned a farm to enter into partnership with one or more of his grown sons or sons-in-law and rent—or preferably buy—a nearby farm. The house on the newly acquired farm often provided a home for the new partner and his family. The greater acreage justified the purchase of larger and more modern machinery, and the greater crop production supported a much larger dairy herd. Most of these farmers built new barns or milking parlors or extensively remodeled existing barns to equip them to meet the higher sanitary standards required to sell their milk to Grade A bottlers. Grade A milk was sold directly for human consumption, and the farmer received an appreciably higher price than was paid to producers of Grade B milk, which was collected and stored under less exacting conditions of cleanliness and sanitation.[2] Grade A milk generally passed directly from the milking machine through pipes and filters to a large refrigerated bulk storage tank. Cleanliness of the barn and milk house and the milking procedures and equipment was strictly enforced by unannounced inspections and testing of the milk for dirt and bacteria. Our farm produced Grade B milk, which was sold to a nearby cheese factory, as Grandpa and Grandma had done for many years. Modernizing our century-old barn to bring it up to Grade A standards would have been very expensive, and the barn was too small for a large dairy herd. Dad never made the transition to Grade A milk production, although he did eventually build a milk house and switch to storing milk in a bulk cooler.

The real key to the prosperity of our most successful neighbors was their willingness to borrow large sums to double or triple the land they farmed and to modernize their buildings and machinery. And the key to managing the increased workload of such an expanded dairy farm was having a willing and committed partner—most often a son or son-in-law.[3] Thus, by the mid-1950s, my brother and I had made decisions that determined the future demise of our family farm, although neither of us foresaw that at the time.

Steve left home first. After graduation from high school in 1955 he enrolled for a year at the University of Illinois in Champaign-Urbana, some 220 miles southeast of our farm. He thought he might like to become a vo-ag teacher, so he enrolled in the College of Agriculture. He enjoyed the social life of a college town, but wasn't very stimulated by many of his courses. After a year he dropped out. For the following two years he lived at home but worked full-time for a lumberyard. He paid my parents for room and board and contributed his labor when he wasn't at his job and Dad urgently needed his help. During this time be began dating Dorleen Showers, whom he had known in high school. In June of 1957 they announced their engagement and a year later they were married. Steve was twenty and Dorleen was nineteen, not uncommon ages for rural couples in our community to marry in those days. They rented an apartment in Freeport and both had jobs. Steve had left home.

Eventually, he became a self-taught agricultural engineer specializing in farm structures, and he operated the buildings division of a large builder's supply company. He designed farm and small industrial buildings, figured out the materials and costs needed to construct them, bid the projects to prospective customers, and supervised the crews who erected the buildings. It proved to be a successful career. He and Dorleen and their son Joel lived in Freeport for over forty years. They were near their parents' farms and helped them in many ways through the years, but Steve left the family farm permanently in June of 1958.

My own departure was more gradual, but no less complete. I graduated from Orangeville High School in 1957 and enrolled at the University of Illinois that fall. I was slightly intimidated by the large and notoriously tough university and my brother's unsatisfactory career there. I had visited the Illinois campus several times on activities sponsored by my high school agriculture classes. The campus and glimpses of college life entranced me. The green lawns and mature trees, the graceful brick Georgian buildings, the overheard intellectual conversations of the students seemed a dream world to me. Fortunately, attendance at the state university was relatively inexpensive. I had earned a county scholarship that paid tuition and fees for all four years by competitive examination given at the Stephenson County courthouse. I still had to find the means to pay for room and board, books and incidentals, which at that time came to about $1,200 a year. My parents agreed to pay me $600 for working on our farm for each summer, and Grandpa Charlie, who lived very frugally and had accumulated his savings, gave me the rest. I supplemented my income with part-time jobs in various kitchens and later as a teaching assistant in the Chemistry Department, but I was able to carry my intensive chemistry major as a full-time student.

I lived at home and worked on the farm during the summers of 1957, 1958, and 1959. During the summers of 1960 and 1961, I remained on the Illinois campus conducting research under a program sponsored by the National Science Foundation and working as a teaching assistant. In August of 1961 I moved to Berkeley, California to begin my studies for the Ph.D. in biochemistry. During the graduate school years I was completely financially independent from my family because I was supported by a fellowship. After the fall of 1959, I only returned to the farm for short visits and no longer contributed significantly to the farm's labor. Mom and Dad were on their own.

During the summers from 1957 through '59 Dad and I worked quite well together. I was physically mature and strong enough for any task. I knew well what needed to be done and how to do it. More importantly, I was earning funds for my goal: a college education. I was on the path to the career I had dreamed of. Although neither I nor anyone in Orangeville High School knew it in 1957, the University of Illinois happened to be one of the finest institutions in the world to study chemistry. My professors were distinguished researchers and many were excellent teachers. My courses were very challenging, but I was fascinated with them and earned excellent grades. I had become aware that generous federal support for science education in the post-Sputnik era would allow me to pursue a Ph.D. without depending on family support or borrowing money. The farm had lost its grip; the path to a career lay open; my old rebelliousness was no longer appropriate.

During the summers the bulk of my work was in the fields, which I preferred to more repetitive chores such as milking cows, feeding hogs, mending fences, or other repairs. However, Dad always saved one especially unpleasant task for my return from college in late May—castrating pigs. The hogs had to be rounded up, caught by the legs, and held immobile on their sides for the surgery, which was without anesthesia. The pigs were frightened and in pain. They should have been castrated much sooner, as they were now big and strong. I had never learned to use the knife, so I was the one who caught and held them down. By the end of a day of wrestling with squealing pigs, my hands were rubbed raw by rough pigskin and my arms and back ached. (My older brother was smarter; he learned to "cut" the pigs as a teenager and got to take turns with Dad holding the porcine victims.)

The summers passed quickly. I often also helped my mother with garden work and canning. We sometimes talked about college, but my emphasis on chemistry and her prior education in biology left us with gaps in discussions of my intellectual pursuits. There was little free time, but I usually went out with friends on Saturday nights to go bowling, see movies, and drink beer in Wisconsin, where the legal drinking age was only eighteen. During the summer of 1959, Grandpa Charlie lived with us for a few weeks while he recovered from one of his hospitalizations for leg ulcers. The old man puttered around the house and buildings, but no longer did farm work. Sometimes he would tell stories of his early life and his adventures out West at the turn of the century. I wish now that I had asked him many more questions and encouraged him to write down his stories, but a young man is too self-absorbed to recognize how interesting his older relatives are and how much they have to teach him.

Grandpa's hospitalization set him to thinking about the

future of the farm, and in 1959 he sold it to my parents for a sum far below its market value so as to avoid estate taxes.[4] Owning a farm without a burdensome mortgage placed my parents in the most financially secure position they had even known. However, important questions about the future of the farm had to be addressed. During the 1960s many of the more successful farmers in the area began buying and renting neighboring farms and doubling or tripling the size of their croplands and dairy herds. Often these expansions required purchase of much larger and more expensive machinery and the renovation or building of new barns. Would my parents join this trend toward expansion and greater modernization? This issue came to a crisis when Dad was offered a chance to buy the farm that lay immediately to the north of ours. The land lay compactly against ours. It would double the size of our farm. The farm's buildings were old and deteriorated; its house would have to be extensively improved to make it desirable for a hired man and his family. A major expansion of the dairy herd would require a new barn or other expensive improvements. A large mortgage would be required. Mother was adamantly opposed. "You can't keep up with the work you have now," she told my father. "How can you handle so much more? Where will we find a good hired man? Young men are leaving the farms for better and easier jobs in the city." Both of my parents were children of the Depression and feared debt. The opportunity passed, and the future of our farm was settled, although I doubt that the finality of the outcome was felt so clearly at the time.

After my departure in 1959, Dad tried to maintain the same farming operation as before by hiring young men to work with him. Several came and went. Most were quite young and still in high school, just out of high school, or dropouts. They lived at home and drove to our farm. Most failed to meet Dad's standards for hard work, reasonable problem-solving skills, and reliability. However, two young men, twin boys still in high school, worked for Dad during summers and distinguished themselves as excellent farm workers. The Scheider boys, John and Jim, were from a large farm family and knew their work well. They also had bright, pleasant personalities. Jim decided that he would accept my parent's offer to live in our big house during the summer so that he wouldn't have to spend so much time driving to and from home. It became clear from my visits home and letters sent to Berkeley that Jim had awakened Mother's maternal instincts. Polite, sweet-tempered, and hard working, he became a favorite of my parents. They enjoyed their talkative mealtimes and rare leisure together. It was not a durable solution to their labor problems, however. When Jim completed high school, he left for college.

As the 1960s passed Dad stopped trying to hire young men and began to reduce his operation. He cut his workload by selling the hogs and concentrated on his dairy business. This proved to be an economically sound decision. Since 1949, the federal government had attempted to stabilize the price farmers received for milk at 75 to 90 percent of "parity" through purchases of surplus dairy products.[5] It was not practical to store milk itself, of course, so butter, nonfat dry milk, and American cheese were purchased. Quotas on the importation of dairy products were also imposed. From 1949 to 1966, milk price supports were fairly stable at 3 to 4 dollars per hundred pounds, but they rose steeply in the 1970s to $7 in 1976, $11 in 1980, and leveled off at $13 during 1981–84.[6] There was no price support program for hogs, and prices were unpredictable and generally less profitable. Dad could raise all of the feed for his cows and calves on the farm and sell any excess corn (for which prices were also federally subsidized). He also began to rent some of his fields to neighboring farmers, usually on a sharecrop basis, sometimes for cash rent. Nonetheless, the relentless cycle of milking cows twice a day, of plowing and planting, harvesting oats and hay and corn, and the oscillations between hot summers and long cold winters went on, year after year.

My mother's workload was decreased during this time as well, because she and Dad stopped planting a big garden and canning homegrown vegetables. Caring for such a big garden and canning by herself had become too great a burden. With their hungry sons no longer at home, the family's food requirements were diminished and could be met with supplies from grocery stores. The farm's apple, plum, and cherry trees continued to provide fruit, which Mother now usually stored frozen. The trees gradually lost their productivity, grew old and gnarled, and died. My parents didn't replace them.

I am embarrassed now to reflect on how little I was involved in my parents' lives during those years. After 1961 I only visited them once a year. I was pursuing a Ph.D. in Berkeley and loving it. Life in Berkeley and the San Francisco Bay area was rich and fascinating. Mother wrote letters faithfully every week, usually on a Sunday afternoon; my replies were far less frequent. When my brother Steve served in the Army from 1961 to 1963 he also received Mother's letters regularly, and recalls how beautifully written they were. Unfortunately, very few of these letters survive. Mother was a skillful writer and managed to construct an entertaining narrative out of the most unpromising material: daily chores and field work, antics of the pets and farm animals, visits with neighbors or letters from friends, comments on world affairs. Some weeks she would not have been away from the farm for the whole time. I believe that she was often unhappy during those years, but she rarely spoke of it.

Another wonderful event distracted me from my parents' faraway rural life. In 1964 I met Bonnie George in Berkeley, and my life was transformed. Within a few months we were happily in love and decided to marry. In the early spring of 1965, we invited my parents to come to California for a holiday, promising to serve as hosts for a tour of many sites we had come to love. To my surprise, they agreed to come, found someone to milk the cows, and booked a flight from Chicago to San Francisco. They later admitted that they were motivated in part by their desire to meet Bonnie so they could feel confident that I had chosen wisely. It turned out to be an island of pleasure in a sea of hard work for them. They were amazed by commercial air flight— the speed and comfort with which they could travel 2,300 miles, leaving wintry Illinois and stepping out into sunny California. They had not been away from the farm overnight, with the exception of hospitalizations, since 1946.

When we arrived at their motel in the morning, Mother had carefully made the bed; she had no idea that a maid would do it while they were out for the day. We toured San Francisco, where cherry blossoms were blooming in Golden Gate Park; crossed the Golden Gate Bridge to Muir Woods with its giant redwood trees; ate in a Chinese restaurant and a favorite Berkeley restaurant. Bonnie prepared a dinner and we invited our friends, mostly fellow Berkeley graduate students, to meet my parents. As I was confident they would, my parents became quickly comfortable with Bonnie. She was charmed by my father and found my mother warm, if a bit shy. She admitted later that she was shocked at how old Mother looked; the years of poor health had taken a gradual toll that I hadn't noticed. During one of our conversations, Dad expressed some of his views on marriage,: "People will say that you have to share the burdens of married life equally," he said, "but I say that you have to carry as much as you can, even if it's much more than the other." Over the years Bonnie and I have wondered if he was describing his own experience in marriage. Probably he felt that he had indeed borne a much heavier load than Mother. If she felt criticized by Dad's comments, she didn't show it, but Bonnie felt uncomfortable for her. It was the beginning of a special rapport that allowed them to be quite close for the rest of Mother's life, even though they had quite different personalities.

Dad and Mom returned to their farm, the twice-daily milking chores, and the annual crop cycle. When Bonnie and I were married in Berkeley in June of 1965, Dad was too busy with fieldwork for my parents to come to the wedding. We visited them on the farm during a long trip in August. The following year I completed my Ph.D. in biochemistry and accepted a postdoctoral fellowship for research at the National Institutes of Health in Bethesda, Maryland. Bonnie and I packed our meager possessions and traveled across the country by car in August of 1966. Again, we stopped at the family farm, this time with the news that we were expecting a child. We settled in Rockville for the two-year duration of my research work at the NIH. It was an extraordinarily exciting and stimulating period for me scientifically, but a time of very tight finances because Bonnie was no longer teaching and my fellowship barely covered our living expenses.

Our son Brian was born in February 1967. He was my parents' first grandchild. We talked by telephone and sent photos. Mother's letters glowed with pleasure. She and Dad did not see their grandson, however, until that summer, when they drove from Orangeville to Maryland and combined a visit with us and Bonnie's parents with a visit to Dad's brother Homer's family and an old college friend of mother's in Virginia. The plan to drive so far was not a good one. My parents were not accustomed to such long driving trips and became irritated and fatigued. Mother had never learned to drive a modern automobile and was not used to reading maps. They arrived after dark in the urban sprawl and dense traffic around Washington, D.C., and became completely lost. Mother became quite ill during their visit to my aunt and uncle's home. She recovered and they made their way home, happy to have seen us and baby Brian, but they never again attempted a long driving trip.

In the spring of 1968 I accepted a position as an assistant professor of biochemistry at my alma mater, the University of Illinois at Urbana. I knew the university well, of course, and I was delighted to have such a splendid professional opportunity. I had never dared to dream of such a wonderful outcome back in my undergraduate days. We moved to Urbana at the end of August 1968. Bonnie had never lived in the Midwest nor set eyes on Champaign-Urbana, but we happily settled in and have lived in Urbana ever since. Our new home brought us closer to the home farm, and we visited my parents regularly during school holidays, typically three or four times a year. Since Steve and Dorleen lived near the farm in Freeport, we visited them too. Bonnie came to experience more of my parents' life on the farm, and she and my mother developed a deeper relationship. Although Mother was a rather private person who shared her feelings only sparingly, she was quite open with Bonnie. It was clear that she was unhappy with life on the farm, but didn't feel that she had any alternatives. She took pleasure in her grandson, however, and in her granddaughter, Stephanie, after she was born to Bonnie and me in May of 1969.

Bonnie and I and Steve and Dorleen combined resources to buy our parents their first television set for Christmas in 1970, a small black and white Zenith. They could receive a few regional stations with reasonably good picture quality. They installed it in the otherwise little-used front parlor. The TV brought the news and much more entertainment into my parents' lives. Mother became fond of a number of afternoon soap operas and carefully reserved times to watch her favorites; they weren't much for intellectual stimulation, but they did bring some amusement into Mother's rather drab and lonely life. Dad watched television relatively little because he was often so tired from the day's chores and fieldwork that he fell asleep in front of it. He complained that the newscasts had a liberal bias.

Brian's memories of this time, formed when he was eight years old and younger, are rich in evocative detail. Years later he wrote:

My earliest memories of the farm are visceral, forever woven together with smells, tastes, and textures: the smell of cinnamon rolls baking in the kitchen, the taste of the sweet dark filling revealed as the roll was pulled apart, a hug from my grandmother, the feel of layers of fragile thin cloth covering the frail, slight woman that she was. There was an odd abandoned, slightly sour smell in the parlor where a TV set would, when occasionally switched on, show a small dark picture of a soap opera after a minute or two. As the World Turns *was my grandmother's favorite, and although I only rarely caught a glimpse, I distinctly remember the image of a slowly revolving planet. I recall the rough fabric of the overstuffed easy chair, worn threadbare by my grandfather, the sticky plastic cover on the table in the living room, the musty smell of the rough lumpy hard mattress in the room that had been my father's, where the wallpaper displayed scientific instruments with a slightly cartoony, demented look to them. And, of course, there was the smell of cow manure, and the hard concrete floor in the barn, where my grandfather talked loudly to be heard over the noise of the milking machine pump—or to maintain his position as head of the family— and the smell of the fresh milk in the gleaming stainless steel cooler in the small milk room with its permanently wet floor.*

My memories of my grandmother are as faint and fragile as I remember her to be, although it may be that the color of my memories has changed her presence over time. She had long silver hair usually tied in a tight bun at the back of her head, but I remember once seeing her standing at a desk in the living room—where a mirror decorated with various odds and ends and my childhood drawings hung on the wall–brushing her hair with a silver-handled brush. Her hair was soft and shone in the light. I remember her hugs—and my hugging her tightly around the waist. I remember her faded red checked sundresses and how they flapped in the wind as they hung out back to dry. The rest of my memories are much more vague and undoubtedly linked to photographs in the family album. Memories of my grandfather are weak at the beginning, but grow stronger as I grew older. I was always fascinated by his size: his huge thick hands, shaped by years of farm work, his great stature and strong head, and his loud voice that could be sharp like a dog's bark. He was always a presence that cast a shadow on the surroundings.

When we first began visiting the farm together, Bonnie was a bit shocked by the primitive farm kitchen and laundry. Mother was still cooking on a wood- and coal-burning kitchen range and washing dishes in metal pans. Washdays were the same daylong struggle with the old-fashioned wringer washer and outdoor clotheslines used in 1951. The kitchen and washhouse were deteriorating, and were especially unpleasant in winter. In 1972, my parents finally decided to tear the old kitchen down and replace it with a modern structure. They planned a large farm kitchen and a laundry-storage room with a automatic washer and clothes dryer. Plans were drawn and contracts set with local builders.

In the late summer of 1972 I received an alarmed letter from Mother. The contractor was scheduled to begin digging trenches and placing forms for the foundations of the new kitchen on Monday of the following week. By then, the old kitchen and washhouse had to be emptied of all their contents and the old one-story wing razed, since the new kitchen would be built in place of the old one. Mother had begun removing everything she could from the kitchen, but Dad was so preoccupied with his fieldwork and milking the cows twice a day that little progress had been made. Mother was in a panic that the contractors would arrive and find the old kitchen still standing. I got on the phone to my brother Steve. "The Old Man has done it again," I said. He quickly agreed that we had to rescue the situation and proposed that he get a couple of his friends to help the two of us do the job on the coming Friday and Saturday.

When I arrived by car Friday afternoon, Steve and his friends had already helped Mother move her refrigerator into the living room and set up an improvised kitchen in a pantry in the main part of the house. She would cook on a hotplate and wash dishes in the bathtub for the next few weeks. They had backed Dad's truck up to the kitchen door and were moving the contents of the washhouse into it. This involved not only heavy items such as the cast-iron kitchen range, the ancient washing machine, and a kerosene stove, but all sorts of accumulated junk in boxes and coffee cans. Dad, like Grandpa Charlie, saved everything on the grounds that it "might come in handy some day." Dad was unnerved by the speed with which we carried it all out and stored it in various outbuildings. He wanted to supervise and organize the operation, but soon saw that he was actually impeding it. He gave up and went to the barn. By evening we had completely emptied the kitchen and washhouse and had begun cutting the connections between the kitchen and the main two-story portion of the house.

The next morning we set to work again. Using the big hydraulic endloader mounted on the front of Dad's tractor (known in our family as the "pooper scooper"), we crushed portions of the walls, pulled away great sections of the roof and walls, and dragged them up to the gravel pit and burned them. The old kitchen had been poorly built. Its foundation beams were flimsy and rotted. The chimney collapsed after a single nudge from the endloader. Within a few hours the old building was removed. Even the stone foundation walls were pulled away with surprising ease. By the end of the day, a strange gap replaced the kitchen that had been so much a part of my childhood and youth. The site was ready for the contractor to lay the new foundations. The speed and thoroughness of our work left my parents a bit stunned, but Mother was very grateful. I think Dad was too, but his feelings were mixed with embarrassment at having been bailed out by his sons and their friends. After a long hot bath and good night's sleep, I drove back to my family in Urbana.

The next time we visited the farm was at Thanksgiving in November of 1972. The new large and brightly lit kitchen had built-in counters and cupboards. A modern sink stood below an attractive window looking out to the yard and orchard. An electric stove replaced Mother's old wood-burning range. Unfortunately, my parents had elected not to install a dishwasher, probably because of the farm's very hard water, although a water softener would have solved that problem. In place of the old washhouse section was a pleasant room with a new clothes washer and dryer.

Since it was to serve as the main entry from the barnyard, the room had a shower and sink for cleanup and a big closet for chore clothes. For the first time in their lives, my parents were able to enjoy the comforts of a modern farm kitchen and laundry—comforts that most families had taken for granted for many years. At first, Mother could hardly believe how easy laundry had become. She tended to visit the washer frequently and hover over the dryer. Could these devices really do automatically what had always taken so much work before? The new kitchen had been well insulated and new ducts from the furnace were installed, so it became the warmest and most comfortable room in the house. My parents spent much of their remaining lives there, Dad especially so in the years after Mother died.

It might have been expected that the new kitchen and modern laundry would have brought greater contentment to my parents, especially to my mother. But perhaps it catalyzed a recognition that they needed to think more seriously about retirement. Mother was sixty-five years old and her health, never good, was fragile. Although she said little about it to us, we came to realize that she became more and more depressed over the following year. Dad was sixty-one and still quite vigorous, but he had developed painful arthritis in his knees from years of squatting under cows and riding rough farm machinery. Mother hoped that he would sell his dairy herd and give up active farming. She never articulated it to me, but I think she really wished that they would sell the farm and retire to a more modern small house in a nearby town. Dad resisted any such radical changes in their lives. He had a point. Although they had no debts and some modest savings, mostly assets inherited from Grandpa Charlie, he felt that they could not get by without their substantial monthly income from the sale of milk. I think he also dreaded the inactivity of living in town. He wanted to stay actively engaged in the only life he knew—farming. He owned the farm; he was in charge there; he needed that sense of autonomy and control. My parents' view of their future was divergent.

During the winter of 1972, Mother began pulling on heavy outdoor clothing and going out to the barn to stay with Dad during the dark cold evenings while he milked the cows. She was not strong enough to be of much help to him, but she felt ashamed to sit in the warm kitchen while he labored alone in the cold barn. She came to the barn mostly to keep him company. It was a kind gesture, but one that she came to regret. The chores took a long time, and the barn was cold and drafty and stank of manure. One could only pet the cats and calves for so long; it was boring. Dad sometimes asked Mother to carry pails of milk that were too heavy for her. She felt useless and wished to be back in the warm house. However, she now felt obligated to keep going to the barn every winter evening; she felt that Dad would resent her no longer doing it. She was trapped by her own good intentions.

By the following year Mother's depression and sense of futility was growing worse, although we only had glimpses of it from things she said to Bonnie during our visits. The repetitive patterns of their lives continued as before, and there was no prospect of any change. Another long cold winter was coming.

In October of 1973, Bonnie and I and the children had just returned from a trip to see the fall colors and covered bridges of Indiana's Parke County and Turkey Run State Park. My brother telephoned us and wouldn't say exactly what was wrong. "It's bad," he said, "really bad. Just come up right away!" Puzzled and worried, we quickly packed up and drove the tiresome five-hour trip over poor roads to Freeport. There, Steve and Dorleen told us what they had been unwilling to say over the telephone: Mother had attempted suicide. Dad had found her and rushed her to the hospital. She had recovered sufficiently to go home to the farm. We found Mother pale and very subdued, but dry-eyed, sitting with her arms wrapped protectively around her thin body. Gradually her story emerged.

She and Dad had finished breakfast in the kitchen a few mornings earlier. They were listening to a local radio station give news of area families: births, weddings, deaths, and funerals. Among the announcements was the report of the wedding of a young couple they knew slightly. After their honeymoon trip, the announcer said, the couple intended to engage in farming. Suddenly, spontaneously and rarely for her, Mother blurted out bitterly, "I'd rather die than spend another life farming!" Dad was struck as though with a fist. It was a true statement of Mother's feelings, but a cruel rejection of the life he had chosen for them. His face clotted with anger, and he rose from the table and stamped out of the kitchen without a word. He worked angrily at his barn chores for two or three hours.

Mother was immediately overwhelmed with remorse for her bitter, hurtful remark. She knew that Dad's anger would be deep and enduring. They were not a couple with skills at resolving conflicts between them. A layer of cold, silent anger would now only deepen the old impasse over the future of the farm. She felt utterly trapped and hopeless, ashamed at having caused more pain, yet having done so by merely speaking her true feelings. She later said that a great, hopeless darkness overwhelmed her; she felt as though she were enveloped in a black tunnel from which there was no escape. Death, she felt, was preferable to this feeling. So she wrote a suicide note to Dad, took a large overdose of sleeping pills, and lay down on the bed that she had shared with Dad for so many years and waited to die.

When Dad returned to the kitchen, he found Mother's suicide note. (We will never know what the note said, because Dad destroyed it.) Mother was in a semiconscious state, but breathing. Dad quickly carried her to the car and drove at high speed to the Freeport hospital where Mother's stomach was pumped, and she was hospitalized for detoxification. She would survive. She later reported that the family physician, a Roman Catholic, "gave me hell, a real tongue-lashing." She was sent home without having been offered any kind of psychological counseling.

Bonnie and I talked gently and separately with my parents, allowing the story to emerge. Dad was deeply humiliated and angered and could barely speak of what had happened. We coaxed my parents to seek the assistance of a professional psychologist or counselor to deal with Mother's depression and the conflicts between them. Both refused. These matters were too private to share with a stranger. They had no confidence in psychological counseling. Mother's attempt at suicide had been a desperate cry for help; I think she hoped that Bonnie and I would be able to persuade Dad to sell his cows and begin a more comfortable life of retirement. If so, we failed her. In fairness, her wishes may have been financially unrealistic, and they didn't accommodate my father's needs. So the impasse remained. Mother promised the family that she would never do anything like that again, and she didn't—but something died in her soul that fall. That something was hope.

In the years that followed Mother became somewhat more withdrawn, less engaged even with her sons and grandchildren. During this time, I believe, she began to admit to herself some of her unhappy private thoughts: her anger with my father, her disappointment with an uncomfortable and wasted life. She took refuge in her reading and TV programs. She hinted at some of this in oblique comments to Bonnie and me. "He can't read my thoughts, can he?" she asked, without specifying what those thoughts were. We reassured her that only she knew her private thoughts.

Does cancer thrive in the bodies of depressed, unhappy persons? The answer isn't known, but we came to wonder about it when a year later Mother was diagnosed with breast cancer. She underwent a radical mastectomy, which was standard surgical treatment at the time, and was subsequently treated with a rather severe course of X-ray irradiation. It seemed that the cancer had been excised in time. My parents' farm life went on as before.

In 1975 I was awarded a Guggenheim fellowship to support a research sabbatical in Freiburg, Germany. It was to be an exciting adventure for our family. We had never been in Europe. I was the only member of the family who had studied German, but we would all have to learn the language in order to live for a year in the country. Brian and Stephanie were of elementary school age and would attend local schools in Freiburg. The year promised challenges, opportunities for scientific growth, and wonderful cultural enrichment. We made plans excitedly for an early September departure. My parents were proud that I had won such a prestigious fellowship and had such an opportunity, but wondered why we needed to go so far away. We tried to share our fascinating experiences with Mom and Dad by sending frequent letters with descriptions of daily life, the children's school, and our travels. Later we borrowed a tape recorder and sent tapes of our voices, even recording the children reading from German schoolbooks and all of us singing German Christmas songs. We hoped that the sounds of our voices would make us seem closer and put some interest into my parents' drab lives.

By the end of the year we began to receive worrisome

reports that Mother was suffering from back pain. Eventually, her physicians discovered that her cancer had metastasized to her spine, and cancer nodes were found throughout her body. Her case was transferred to an oncologist in Rockford. Her cancer was unresponsive to the milder forms of chemotherapy they attempted, and Mother refused the more drastic forms. She probably had a year to live.

The following March, I flew back from Germany by myself, partly to consult with my research group in Urbana, but mostly to spend some time on the farm with Mother. She was calm, and fortunately not suffering. I drove her to Rockford for one of her visits to her oncologist. She was able to talk very frankly with him about the course of her disease and her prospects for the future. She showed me a list on which she had designated who was to receive her favorite possessions after her death—old family furniture, antique toys and dishes that had been passed down to her from her family. She had made a new will. In her orderly way, she was making final arrangements. It was a calm and relatively unemotional visit, and I returned to Germany with the feeling that her emotional health was good and her physical health was fragile, but stable. The winter had been a difficult one for Dad. Many trips to clinics in bad weather and Mother's growing inability to perform her usual kitchen and household work added to his barn chores, but much of the anger of two years before was gone—what was the point now?

January 1977 was one of the harshest winter months on record in Illinois, both because of the bitter cold and heavy snowfalls. The snow accumulated in great drifts and heaps where the snowplows left it. Mother became so weak that caring for her in the old farmhouse was more and more impractical. Frequent trips to the Rockford clinic in the harsh, snowy weather were a great burden; often it was so cold that Dad couldn't get his car started. By the middle of the month Mother was hospitalized in Rockford. I received a call from my brother urging me to come north because it seemed that she might not live much longer. Bonnie and Brian were both suffering from a miserable throat infection that had resisted antibiotic treatment. The drive to Rockford in such cold and snowy conditions was no pleasure trip, even a bit dangerous, but I headed north alone.

I found Mother in her hospital room, clearly very weak, but calm and reasonably cheerful. She was looking forward to watching the inauguration of President Jimmy Carter on TV—not that she was a Democrat, but she enjoyed such public ceremonies. We talked, and I believe I gave her some comfort and cheer, but neither of us treated the visit as though it were our final reunion. At the end I hurried out because I wanted to ask her doctor some questions before he disappeared down the hall, and I did not return to her room.

The drive alone back to Urbana in extreme cold and blowing, drifting snow and total darkness was an enervating experience. I had been back with my sick family for only a day when Dorleen called in the middle of the night to say that Mother had died. I regretted that we had never properly said goodbye, that I had not told her that I would always be grateful to her for inspiring and encouraging my career in academic science—that her life had *not* been a waste, but a gift. In our reticence to speak of tender and loving feelings we were very typical of farm families of northern European heritage.

It was twenty degrees below zero the morning our sad little family got into our car, Bonnie still suffering from fever and a raging sore throat. We drove through the bitter cold and snow to Freeport and to the farm. We stumbled through the rituals of death in rural America: visitation at the funeral home, the grotesque practice of an open casket, a religious service that meant nothing but false promises to me, following the hearse to a frozen cemetery, and then a large gathering at the family farmhouse where friends and relatives ate food brought by neighbors and enjoyed a reunion. Two months before her seventieth birthday, Mother left the farm forever for a cold grave. Dad was alone.

Winter mood on
the farm.

Chapter Five

The Long Twilight (1977–1991)

The technological and economic forces that transformed American agriculture after World War II intensified during the final three decades of the twentieth century. The trend toward consolidation of small farms continued. The number of farms in the United States declined by 381,000 from 1975 to 1990; the number of people living on farms fell from 8.8 million to 4.6 million during the same period.[1] Farmers responded to economic pressures by planting ever-increasing acreages or, in the case of livestock farmers, by factory farming of beef cattle, hogs, poultry, and dairy herds on a very large scale. Alternatively, smaller farms relied on jobs away from the farm; by 2002, 93 percent of farm households had off-of-the-farm income.[2] The economic security of farmers was undermined by overproduction, which was driven by their increasing efficiency and ever-improving technology. This situation fueled an ongoing debate over farm price support programs, production controls, and export policies.[3]

To a substantial extent, Dad's senescing farm stood aside from these sweeping changes. He continued to live on the farm alone for another fourteen years. He never considered any other possibility. After thirty-one years, the farm had become his home, his life, the place where he was comfortable and was in charge. He owned the farm outright; his standard of living did not require a large net income. A gregarious man, he must have been lonely at times, but leaving the farm would have been too high a price to pay for company. For the first few years after Mother died, he continued to farm as he had before. He kept his dairy herd and milked cows twice a day. He did some of the fieldwork and rented the rest of his land to neighboring farmers. As the years passed, his ability to manage the workload gradually diminished. Painful arthritis made his milking chores difficult and slow. During a bad winter sometime in the early 1980s, he realized that it was no longer safe for him to maintain a dairy herd alone. Whether this realization was brought about by a specific disturbing incident, he didn't say. If he were to fall or be knocked down by an obstreperous cow, he might lie in need of medical assistance in the cold barn for a very long time—days even—before any one would be aware of the situation. The following summer, during a period of good prices for dairy cows, he sold the entire herd to another farmer. He kept his heifers for another year and sold them when they were expecting their first calves. It was a major step in his acceptance of a life of retirement. In his last years on the farm, the only remaining animals were a group of semi-feral cats living in the barn. Even though he had never been very fond of cats, Dad prepared a mix of warm milk and rolled oats (a cheap form of oatmeal) and fed it to the cats twice daily. "I have to feed my livestock," he'd say jokingly. The routines of daily chores were so deeply engrained into his life that he needed this little chore for his sense of well-being. One of my enduring memories from the late 1980s is of Dad surrounded by eager cats, their tails high, as he walked slowly with very bowed arthritic legs to the barn carrying his pail of cat food.

His tenderness with the cats did not extend to veterinary services, however, and they were sometimes a scabby, diseased-looking lot and suffered a high mortality rate.

Relieved of his chores and gradually doing less and less work in the fields, Dad had the time—and, as it turned out, the money—to make some much-needed repairs to his house and buildings. The house especially needed attention. Mice could be heard scrambling and squealing in the walls at night. During one of our visits we prepared for bed in the upstairs room only to discover that mice had laboriously carried hundreds of kernels of seed corn from an adjacent room and tucked them between the sheets at the foot of our bed. Commercial seed corn is coated with powdery pink insecticide, which stained the sheets (and probably poisoned the mice). Fortunately, Bonnie was able to locate clean sheets left by my mother, and remade the bed. The roof of the house had begun to leak badly around the unused chimneys. During one of our visits to the farm it rained heavily, and we were kept awake all night by the sound of water dripping into buckets and pails in our upstairs bedrooms. The walls and ceilings were soaked and stained; the wallpaper fell away from them in great sheets. The poor old house sustained considerable damage before Dad arranged to have the chimneys removed, the roof repaired, and new shingles and gutters installed. Later he had the house, barn, and outbuildings repainted. Steve and I paid for decorative shutters on the façade of the house, and Steve helped Dad install them. The original, very worn wood shingles on the barn were replaced with new wood shingles. This was much more expensive than asphalt shingles or metal roofing—Steve said Dad might as well have used dollar bills for shingles—but it was a measure of his respect for the old Pennsylvania Dutch barn, especially when one considers that he no longer used the barn for cattle.

During the 1980s, the most severe debt foreclosure crisis since the Great Depression overwhelmed a substantial minority of American farmers.[4] Stimulated by good farm prices in the previous decade, which were fueled in part by rising exports of farm products, pervasive inflation, and easy credit, many farmers went deeply into debt to acquire or enlarge farms and to invest in machinery and modern buildings. Farm debt (in constant dollars) increased by 59 percent from 1970 to 1980.[5] Farmland prices soared in Iowa—from $834 per acre in 1974 to $2147 in 1981.[6] Farmers relied on the rapidly increasing value of their farms to amortize their debt. The "farm bubble" burst in the early 1980s; among the causes were very high interest rates, decreased exports due to embargoes and the high dollar, and a shift in the policy of the Federal Reserve to restrict inflation.[7] Farmland values plummeted; from 1982 to 1987 the value of U.S. farm assets dropped by 31 percent, more than $300 billion.[8] Foreclosures on farm mortgages rose sharply. Many farmers lost their farms, sometimes farms that had been in their families for many decades. The pain was not distributed uniformly, however. Younger, more ambitious farmers often incurred the largest debt. Some 63 percent of farm debt in 1984 was owed by only 19 percent of farmers.[9] Naturally, it was these farmers who were in the most trouble.

Following the nationwide trend, some of Dad's neighbors had borrowed heavily to expand their farms, build modern barns, silos, and machine sheds, and buy expensive new machinery to speed up their fieldwork. Dad watched this process with some feeling of resentment. He had been unwilling to accept the risks of debt needed to expand; his sons had not wanted to continue operating the family farm; his time of opportunity to become one of the more visibly prosperous and successful farmers in the area had passed. Some of his neighbors were "getting too big for their britches," as he put it, and he disapproved of their prideful behavior. Back in 1976, when it became generally known that Mother was dying, one of our adjacent neighbors approached Dad about buying his farm. Dad refused and never forgave the insensitivity and opportunism he felt had accompanied the offer. When the farm debt crisis in the 1980s developed, some neighboring farm families were overwhelmed by unsecured debt. One neighbor who lost his farm committed suicide. More fiscally secure farmers gobbled up the failed farms and increased their holdings. The economist Neil Harl summarizes Dad's situation neatly: "Those who were the least impacted were not necessarily the most efficient and, in fact, tended to be the older, more cautious farmers with slightly smaller operations and little or no debt."[10] Dad watched the failures with grim satisfaction.[11] Thanks to his fiscal conservatism, he would never risk losing his farm and possessions to debt. He must have been aware, however, that his family farm would eventually cease to exist as the result of less dramatic—but no less relentless—economic forces.

Dad visited us in Urbana only very infrequently, perhaps a half-dozen times, in the fourteen years after Mother died. Our usual pattern was to visit him for a few days on the farm about three times a year, as school holidays permitted. These visits usually occurred during spring break, once or twice during the summer, and at Thanksgiving or Christmas. I always disliked the winter visits because the house was so cold and uncomfortable, and we were in danger of encountering winter storms that could leave us stranded on the farm or on the road. My old, irrational fear of being trapped would return when snowstorms threatened. By contrast, the summer visits were the most pleasant. Before Dad sold the cows we were wakened early in the morning by his calling them to the barn. The musical calls of meadowlarks, bobolinks, and red winged blackbirds living in the sunny fields around the house sweetened the mornings. I helped Dad with his milking chores, although I often wondered if I made the job take longer because we talked so much—not of personal things, which Dad didn't address comfortably, but he was interested in the world of ideas and in my experiences and opinions as an academic scientist who often traveled in Europe. Our political ideas had diverged a great deal over the years. Dad wanted to know what I thought and listened to my liberal philosophy without emotion, but I don't think he changed many of his own opinions. He had a remarkable memory of such odd topics as the order of ascent to the throne of various families of English monarchs, lines from Shakespeare's plays, and scraps of French poetry. Occasionally we arrived at haymaking time, and I joined in. Our children got to see that their father was still competent enough to load bales and operate a tractor and a hay baler.

Brian and Stephanie have many memories of their visits to Grandpa's farm during these years that reflect a different and more positive perspective than mine. I excerpted the following from a collection of Brian's memories.

* * * * *

Although I have no evidence of it, I have the feeling that our visits to the farm grew less frequent after grandma died. We still visited once or twice a year during the warmer times of year. My sister and I looked forward to the visits for their novelty. These were years of adventure on the farm. In addition to the house with its hidden rooms full of dusty things, the farm had the barn and several outbuildings to explore. The sheds were filled with all manner of farm equipment, animals, and supplies—or, as my father said, junk. My great grandfather and my grandfather had a tendency to keep everything. Rather than throw things away, unused objects were taken to the gravel pit. The gravel pit was a great gash in a hillside that resembled a Greek amphitheatre. It had once been a quarry, and there were still limestone chunks lying around, many with fossils. There was always something to see and discover, an endless supply of adventure for a young boy. In the gravel pit was everything that the farm had worn out over the years: an old wooden silo that had been turned into hog houses (complete with desiccated hog droppings), twisted trees, hunks of concrete, machinery of all shapes and sizes, wagon parts, wood, nails, bolts, wire, strange jars of odd liquids. In the summer a depression at one end filled with rainwater, and the pond became home to algae, frogs, toads, snakes, and the occasional muskrat. At first my father and sister and I would explore together, and later as we grew older I would explore alone or with my sister and my cousin Joel. In the winter we crunched through the snow and scaled the steep sides of the quarry, enjoyed the view of the farm, slid down again on our coats, built castles and forts of snow, had snowball fights, waited quietly to try and see a muskrat, crunched ice under our boots until our feet got cold and our faces were red from the cold biting wind. For my sister and me the farm became synonymous with these adventures. Even the trip up to the farm (a hard five-hour drive on beat-up two-lane roads with unusual tensions between my parents, which I only understood years later) was full of sights that were otherwise unseen in my life in Urbana.

My cousin Joel was the youngest of the three grandchildren and, although he is now a great giant of a man, I will always remember him as the little tagalong. He always had a mischievous twinkle in his eye and a knack for getting into trouble. One Sunday my Uncle Steve, my Aunt Dorleen, and cousin Joel came for a visit to the farm. They were all dressed up, and Joel had on nice pants and new saddle shoes. Since it was a nice sunny day, Steph, Joel, and I went out to play with the farm cats (a gaggle of mixed-breed, sour, stray and unkempt critters that lived off of kitchen scraps, milk, and mice) and poke around. It wasn't long before Joel stepped in a fresh cow pie, sinking into it over the tops of his new shoes. While the three of us found this amusing and giggled as Joel squished towards the house, Aunt Dorleen was aghast and after a scolding they left rather abruptly.

One hot summer day, when we were old enough to go to the quarry alone, we went exploring there. We wore t-shirts and jeans and went to look at the pond with the vague idea of building a raft. The pond had received droppings and churning from the cows, and in the hot summer it was filled with green algae and brown scum and tadpoles. We were trying to build a raft, but it wasn't going well, and Joel was either in the way or splashing water. Someone threw a fistful of wet algae at Joel, creating a huge green splotch on his clean white t-shirt. Before long we were all knee deep in the pond and slinging dripping hunks of algae at each other, laughing and shouting. Later, wet and tired, we slopped back to the farmhouse to present ourselves. We were all a mess. Joel even had hunks of algae stuck in his blond hair and earned an extra helping of parental outrage.

Eating at the farm was also an adventure of sorts. The kitchen was focus of almost all activity in the house. There were three meals every day, almost always on the thick utilitarian plastic plates of various somber colors. If the meal was for a special occasion, we used the Fiestaware, which was in deep blue and cream colors, but somewhat more ornate and cheery. Fitting to a dairy farm, every meal had ample amounts of fresh milk, butter, and thick slabs of cheese from the local cheese maker. The emphasis was on simplicity and plenty. The food was hearty and good, but never fancy—in some ways like my grandparents. The pantry next to the kitchen was store to an amazing variety of canned and pickled fruits, vegetables, jams, and jellies, which were often used to augment and flavor the meal. I always looked forward to the fresh sweet corn that my grandparents served when it was in season. (I think Midwesterners all are a bit spoiled by the quality of their sweet corn, but most never know it because few ever leave.) The table and chairs were wooden, painted gray, and creaked and wobbled slightly. The meals were often long, and the conversation was filled with a variety of topics of my grandfather's choosing. My father always sat at the opposite end of the table from my grandfather; the rest of us sat on the sidelines and ate.

One epic summer my parents left us with my grandfather while they went to Door County, Wisconsin, for a holiday. This time provided a miniature view of what I imagine childhood to have been like for my father. On the morning following my parents' departure, Steph and I were rudely awakened by a bellow from the base of the steep stairs to the upstairs. "Get up!" was the simple message. Shocked by this new experience, Steph came into my room and asked, "Did you hear that?" We sat in bed in our pajamas like watchful spooked mice. A minute later the door banged open again and the demand was repeated: "Get up! You're gonna get bedsores!" My sister and I just looked at each other. I said, "I guess we better get up." Grandpa had been up since five-thirty to milk his cows. He had made breakfast and was tired of waiting for his lazy grandchildren. Spoiling them wasn't on his mental map. After a surly breakfast we made peace with the matter by not mentioning it again. Steph and I got up earlier from then on. We followed Grandpa around asking him questions, helping as much as we were able with chores, but mostly just watching.

One day we were done early, so he decided to barbeque some

hotdogs for lunch. Hotdogs and an awful, sweet low-cost soft drink were my grandfather's idea of what young people ate; undoubtedly, this was an idea planted by my cousin Joel, who for a time ate only such things. The weenie roast was loads of fun. We had to find wood and a suitable place to start a fire, as well as find and sharpen sticks for roasting the hotdogs. A few buns, ketchup, mustard, pickle relish, and bottles of drink completed the meal. Once the wood was chopped and piled, Grandpa took a box of blue-tip strike-anywhere matches from the chest pocket of his overalls (there always seemed to be something useful in there), and to Steph's and my giggling delight lit a match on the seat of his pants. ("His butt!" my sister would say.) It was a great afternoon, hot sun mixed with food and adventure, and Grandpa in one of his rare sunny moods—a memory to cherish.

Making hay was also an adventure, in spite of my hay fever. The old tractor, hay baler, and old wagons made it seem that time had stopped in the fifties. Farm work had something intrinsically manly about it—field work more so than the rest. Everyone was sweating, it was noisy, and the work was hard and at times dangerous. My father grumbled that it would have been easier if it had been done sooner, if the hay hadn't been rained on. While it lasted it was great fun. Since I was too young to help very much, I was permitted to ride on the wagon back to the hayloft. The great cavernous space above the milking part of the barn always seemed open and grand. Thick wooden beams held together with wooden pegs reached up to the roof. The hayloft was often piled high with warm, scratchy hay and straw. It had a wonderful smell and was a great place to play hide and seek or to pet the cats and find their hidden litters of kittens. Or just to look out of the window at the fields and the farmhouse. It was my favorite place on the farm after the quarry.

The summer Joel was thirteen or fourteen years old, my uncle bought an All Terrain Vehicle for him. This four-wheeled monster had a semi-automatic kick shift and could hit fifty-five miles per hour on a flat stretch. My uncle had tried it out as well, but when we first saw it, he had given it up after trying to climb a steep hill in the quarry and had the ATV land on him. We should have paid more attention to this omen. To my mother's dismay, the three grandchildren tooled around on the thing. Each of us had fun and our share of trouble. I took an unwanted trip through the corner of a field of tall corn (which really hurts at forty miles per hour). Joel was thrown once or twice, but escaped with minor cuts and bruises. One afternoon we went to the back forty acres of the farm where there was a large open field, and took turns riding. The field was rough and uneven. As Steph roared along one edge of a field, she hit a fallen fence post hidden in the grass. She lost control and swerved through a barbed wire fence. Luckily she fell off the ATV as it hit the fence, but her arm took a terrible raking and gaped open in three places near the elbow. I reached her first. She stood staring at her bleeding arm and said, "I feel sick." I stripped off my t-shirt and wrapped her arm—more to stop her seeing the blood than to stop the bleeding. Joel raced to the house to get help. Dad and Grandpa drove up a few minutes later in Grandpa's brown Chevy pick-up, and after a quick explanation from me, they were off to the hospital. One tetanus shot, twenty-seven stitches, and three scars later, the ATV farm adventures had lost their charm.

* * * * *

Dad eventually realized that his eyesight was sharply diminished; he was suffering from the "wet" form of macular degeneration, and, because the disease acts so gradually, his vision was already badly and irreversibly damaged. Treatments arrested some of the deterioration, but by the middle of the 1980s he was legally blind, unable to read anything but very large print. The most devastating effect was that he was forced to stop driving his car and truck on the highways. He caused an accident in which the other driver was injured, fortunately not severely. Dad was shocked into realizing that he had to give up his driver's license. For a farmer who lived alone on a farm that was five miles from the nearest village, this was a serious problem. He could not rely on my brother Steve and his wife Dorleen or the kindness of neighbors for all of his driving. Eventually, he found another retired farmer, Melvin Thomas from Freeport, whom he hired to drive for him. Mel was as arthritic as Dad, but he could see to drive. The two old men shared many common experiences and views of the world, and they gradually became good friends. Mel's driving was supplemented many times by Steve and Dorleen, especially when Dad needed medical treatment in Madison, some sixty miles away, and by Bonnie and me when we were visiting. Taking Dad to the grocery store was a frustrating experience. He had a list, which was illegible to us and read only with great difficulty by him, and he had more or less memorized the location of items in his favorite grocery store. Nonetheless, the selection of items on his list involved a random walk through the store, returning to the same aisles again and again. Dad gave up reading, but was able to derive some pleasure from watching television and listening to taped books for the blind. When we drove through the countryside, I was always surprised at how well he used what little vision he had left. He usually knew where we were and could give directions in areas where I didn't know the roads.

Dad's hearing also got much poorer. By this time, he was in his seventies. The accumulated handicaps were difficult for him, and he often seemed depressed and angry on our visits to the farm. He was tired by nightfall; it was not unusual for him to fall asleep while Bonnie or I were talking to him. He had no reason—other than the habit formed by so many years of milking cows—to rise early, but his radio alarm went off every morning at five-thirty. Loudly. So loudly that it blasted Bonnie and me out of our bed upstairs. I staggered downstairs in search of relief and sometimes found him still sound asleep in spite of the din. More often, he was up and wanted to talk over the radio's deafening racket. By this time, Dad was no longer doing a significant amount of farm work, although he got a riding mower and mowed the grass and weeds around the buildings, repaired fences, and grumbled about the farmer who was renting his fields. His needs were simple and he lived frugally from his rent income. "I have a halfwit I keep around for his room and board," he'd say when joking about the economics of his farm operation.

* * * * *

Stephanie wrote this portrait of her grandfather during this period when she was a senior in high school, in 1986:

My grandfather is a tired man. He's got huge rough hands. Under his fingernails is a lifetime's worth of dirt that will never be removed. Parts of two of his fingers are missing. Cruel accidents happen with hay balers. He hasn't got much hair left, just this white fringe that can be seen beneath his faded seed corn hat. His eyes are a deep blue. But they are no longer clear. A clouded vision blurs his world and infuriates his sense of self-worth. He stoops a little now, and arthritic knees slow his walk. He doesn't milk cows anymore. His calling the cows out of the pasture no longer awakens me early in the morning. The tall corn in the fields isn't his anymore. A neighboring farmer rents the land. He keeps his buildings in good shape, though. The barn was just painted its bright new red. He even had a new roof put on it. All that's in there is hay now. The machine shed is like a museum of farm equipment. Rusted hay cutters, ancient tractors, combines, and even an old truck with his name on the door fill the place. Just the faded white house needs paint. And since my grandmother has been gone, the garden around it has fallen to ruin, and the kitchen no longer smells of freshly baked cinnamon rolls. The house could use some insulation. In the winter the curtains blow with the wind. I can even see my breath sometimes. He doesn't seem to mind, though. He sits at the kitchen table with this head in his hands, leaning over a cup of coffee. The radio blares behind him, but I'm not sure he's hearing it. It's funny, sometimes he doesn't even hear us arrive. It's so rare for a car to come down his lane, you'd think he'd hear us. I guess that's part of aging too.

When I was little I used to carry milk to the cooler for him. We'd go out early in the morning and then again late at night. My special treat was to feed the calves and the cats. Sometimes my dad would come out too. I'd hardly recognize him in the work clothes he wore. He and grandpa would talk. I could never really hear what they were saying. It was a warm feeling out there in the barn. I'd sit on a bale of straw and hold a cat on my lap. I remember once crying over a cat that had been crushed to death by a cow. There aren't many cats left anymore. But grandpa still goes out twice a day to feed them some dried cat food. He talks to them and they climb up his leg onto his shoulder.

Someday he won't be around to feed them anymore. They'll migrate to neighboring farms, I suppose. When I was little I used to think the farm would be there forever. There was a timelessness about it. But I have watched his world darken, and the sounds fade from his ears, and his shoulders slump. I have seen already some of the older buildings crumble and virtually disappear into the tall grass. I have watched the cows go from fifty to ten to, finally, none. I don't want to think that someday he will go too. Then this farm, that holds so many memories for me, will gradually crumble and fade into a skeleton of what it used to be, like so many you see along the highways.

Our son Brian, by now a college student, visited his grandfather by himself occasionally during these years and later recalled:

High school, earning a drivers license, and other rites of young manhood filled my world and distracted me from the farm. Infrequent visits tapered off further. But a college sophomore photography project awakened a new interest in the farm. During a wintry visit I explored the farm with new eyes, visiting my old haunts and shooting rolls of black and white film. I photographed still lives, my father and grandfather while talking, working, or resting. I started to see the farm in a larger context—in relation to the surrounding farms—and it became apparent that my grandfather and his farm were becoming a thing of the past. The Cahoon and Busjahn families had done well and were farming on an industrial scale. On drives through the area we frequently saw farms with five or six massive blue Harvestore silos, where a single smaller concrete silo had been the rule in the past. And we occasionally saw abandoned houses falling into ruin. When I started taking photos, I was more interested in aesthetics, because it was at the start of my studies in design. I selected photos based on looks rather than meaning, printed and mounted them, but they stayed with me and on my mind.

As I continued to study and inherited our family's old Volvo station wagon, I took the opportunity to visit my grandfather on my own. I sometimes took a camera, but not always. Our visits were *now more like that between adult friends; even though I was clearly much younger, Grandpa began to treat me as more of an equal. This changed the dynamic between us. When I arrived tired from the long drive, he met me at the door and stuck out his great hand to shake. I ignored it and took him in my arms—I was now as tall as he was—and held him close. I will never forget his sudden stiffness and then slow, but affectionate pats on the back. When I think about it now, I doubt if he could have given me that hug even if he had wanted to. He had somehow never learned how, but it was okay as long as I initiated it. While I was there we shared everything: meals, cooking, cleaning, stories—whatever there was to do. I helped him sew shirts. My eyes and sewing skills were better than his, but I had to endure his teasing about me making someone a good wife someday. As his eyesight got worse, he lost his driver's license. I drove him into town to run errands: pay bills, go to the bank, buy overalls, or get a haircut. These were mundane but pleasant activities, as if I had always been there. At home one would scarcely notice his impairment because he was so familiar with his surroundings, but he needed help with tasks like dialing a number on the rotary phone in the barn or reading letters.*

It was during one of my solo visits that we went to the back forty acres and to the abandoned house that stood on a neighboring farm adjacent to the field. We talked about who had lived there and about the kids who had broken in and trashed the place. Although he never mentioned it, I could feel his foreboding that this might well be the fate of his farm. Knowing the likely inclinations of my father and uncle on the future of the farm, I shared the feeling too. I poured this emotional energy surrounding the future of my grandfather and the fate of the farm into my art during two years of printmaking at the University of Illinois. Woodcuts and monoprints, some reprinted in this book, sought to capture what I was feeling. I have seldom had such a productive and direct outpouring of creative energy. I greatly enjoyed creating this art, but the fate of the farm weighed heavily on me.

* * * * *

In December of 1989, Dad sought medical attention for symptoms of colon cancer. Unfortunately, the diagnosis was positive. He underwent surgery during a gloomy December afternoon while my brother and I fidgeted and worried in a waiting room. Dad recovered well over the next few days in the hospital and seemed quite cheerful. He was fond of the nurses, mostly young women from the surrounding rural areas. It was a shock to me to see a large sign over his bed: MR. SWITZER IS LEGALLY BLIND. He had always made such good use of his remaining vision in the familiar setting of the farm that we never thought of him as blind, but the nursing staff needed to be aware of his visual handicaps. He returned to the farm and recovered well. Steve and Dorleen began taking him to Madison for regular medical examinations, a trip that they were to take many times over the next two years. It appeared that Dad had dodged a bullet and that his quiet life on the farm alone would continue for a long time.

But within a year an examination brought bad news: his colon cancer had returned, and another surgery was required. The surgery revealed that the cancer was metastatic to his liver and peritoneum. Dad declined aggressive chemotherapy, which did not hold out great promise in any case; he had only a year or two to live.

He took this terrible news quite calmly. He refused to consider leaving the farm for a nursing home, but came to rely increasingly on Steve and Dorleen, who lived nearby, for trips to Madison and for supplies. He shed the depression and submerged anger that had been evident in earlier years, when he was struggling to accept his semi-blindness, his arthritis, and his loss of his once extraordinary strength and self-sufficiency. "I've had a good run," he said. He did not seek the comforts of religion and he made few plans for his coming death other than updating his will. But his connections to his family became a bit softer and gentler. He was especially tender toward his three grandchildren, although he never openly expressed his affection for his sons or their wives.

As Brian recalls those years:

After my graduation from Illinois I went to Boston to work. My life and my pursuit of independence there consumed almost all of my mental space. Life on the farm continued, and Grandpa's health deteriorated slowly. After about two years in Boston I applied to graduate school and was accepted into a program IIT in Chicago. I lived in student dormitories in the middle of one of the worst ghettos in the city, so I was happy to have an excuse to escape the city. I began visiting the farm again. Grandpa was slower now, and I started to ask more questions—about people, his family, and the farm. I taped some of our conversations about the family tree and took notes. I helped him more now than ever. During my studies Grandpa was diagnosed with advanced colon cancer and underwent surgery. Even though he had sworn he would rather die than live with a colostomy bag, which was his fate after the second operation, he somehow made do, as he always had. I gave him some of my artwork and showed him others and the photographs. He saw the work very differently than I did—not as the emotionally laden depiction of a passing world, but simply as literal renderings of ordinary objects and scenes.

We visited from Urbana as often as we could. During one of those visits in the summer of 1991, Dad told Steve that he wanted to have a talk with both of us, an unusual request that suggested to us that he was thinking about the future of our family farm. We drove Dad to get his haircut and waited for him to tell us what was on his mind. He was slow to come to it, anticipating that it might be a difficult conversation. Finally, he spoke his mind. He was indeed thinking of the future of the old farm. He didn't say what we all knew: that it had been in the family for seventy-five years, that it had been our boyhood home, and that it was the home he loved above all others. He did say that he wanted us to keep the farm in the family. Gently, but firmly, we declined. Neither of us had the time or inclination to supervise the farm properly. I lived over two hundred miles away and was very preoccupied with additional obligations as head of the biochemistry department at Illinois. Steve and Dorleen lived much closer, but Steve was also fully occupied with leading the buildings division of J. H. Patterson and Company. The farm was too small and too run-down to support a tenant farmer. It would have to be rented to neighboring farmers and largely unsupervised. The abandoned buildings would be easy targets for thieves and vandals. The farm did not present an attractive site to either of us for a retirement or vacation home. Reluctant as we were to disappoint our dying father, we could not deceive him with false promises. After he was gone, the farm would be sold.

Dad accepted our decision calmly, as though he had been expecting it. "I'm leaving you boys with a mess," he said, thinking of the numerous buildings filled with old machinery and objects and the big old house crammed with the accumulation of seventy-five years. "But you will be well compensated for taking care of it." He had no intention of clearing it out and selling any of it himself.

We never spoke again of the future of our farm.

In April of 1991, only six months before he died, Dad wrote a letter to Bonnie and me in which he unsparingly examined his life:

I realize that I have had many disappointments to myself and those who care/cared for me. I also know that many were caused by my own bad judgment and/or ignorance on my part. Yes, circumstance has a bearing on one's success or failure, and that gives one an excuse. One's personality and ability probably are more important, but those are not always controllable qualities.

I am proud of the job I did of bringing a farm in a very low state of production to a highly productive bit of land and a farm with the erosion highly controlled. From an economic standpoint, as the saying goes, not a viable unit today.

I am glad I am able live in my own home and am highly jealous of my prerogatives. No one can do as he pleases all the time or maybe scarcely ever, but in my own house, there I feel that I am king.

When I was growing up, it was at the end of an era in the agricultural sector. At least, the largest industry was farming and a farm was security. Farmers produced and processed most of their own food, fuel, and bred the animals that produced the meat, milk, and motive power for their agricultural equipment. Since money was not in large supply, most of us lived by the "use it up, wear it out, make it do" philosophy and also often found use for the salvage, like Dolly Parton's "Coat of Many Colors." So with me I have hewn very close to the line of Grandpa: "don't throw it away; it may come in handy." Hence there are a lot of things hereabout which are either junk or valuable antiques.

In 1991, Dad served as the host of the annual Switzer family reunion. His grandfather, W. H. Switzer, and his grandmother, Anne Hawk Switzer, had ten children who grew to adulthood, so Dad had many cousins. A number of years earlier a group of the cousins began holding annual reunions, usually at a home or park in northern Illinois or eastern Iowa, where many family members still lived, even though others were scattered from coast to coast. Dad wanted to host the gathering, but his old farmhouse and cranky plumbing did not provide a suitable site. The reunion was scheduled for August 11, 1991 in Lake Le-Aqua-Na State Park, some fifteen miles from the farm. As a practical matter, Steve and Dorleen did most of the work of sending out invitations and arranging for food and drink (although those relatives who didn't live too far away brought dishes to share). Relatives began arriving on August 10. The reunion was very well attended; I think many of them knew that Dad was dying and they might not see him again. All of Dad's immediate family, including his three grandchildren, was there.

The event was on a bright sunny day with rather cool breezes—perfect for the picnic, children's games, and massive amounts of typical midwestern food. Dad presided happily. As he rose to welcome his many family members and to invite others to stand and share news of their respective branches, I saw more clearly than I had before how ill he was. He was jaundiced from his diseased liver; his once-powerful body was visibly thin and bent, and his once pink and smooth skin hung in loose wrinkles. He could see only vaguely. His shirt bulged where it covered his ostomy bag. But his voice was strong and his spirits were high; he was clearly enjoying his role as host.

Our daughter Stephanie was working that year in a grueling job as a paralegal aide in a large New York City law firm, but she managed to get away for the weekend to attend the reunion along with David Brule Jr., whom she would later marry. She and Dave had to leave early to catch her flight back to New York. I stood at a distance while she said goodbye to Dad. As the only granddaughter, she had always enjoyed Dad's special affection. She was tall, slender, and beautiful. The old man embraced her warmly, and she turned away quickly to hide her tears. She would never see her grandfather again and she knew it.

Scenes from the
farm auction,
November 9, 1991.

Chapter Six

The Family Farm No Longer (September–November 1991)

The family reunion in August was Dad's last day in the sun. After his guests departed, he returned to his quiet life alone on the farm. He could look forward to his eightieth birthday on October 1, 1991, but he didn't live to see it.

At the end of August he suddenly developed severe abdominal pain. He was admitted to the hospital in Freeport, but his condition rapidly deteriorated. Bonnie and I returned to Freeport to visit Dad in the hospital. It was painful to see him. This once massively muscled man lay jaundiced and emaciated in an ill-fitting hospital gown. He knew he was dying, but didn't speak of it directly. He asked for little except for well water from the farm, because he hated the chlorine-flavored water the hospital provided.

What do you say to your dying father? I was awkward, distressed to see him so enfeebled. I had not been emotionally close to my father. We had never been able to express affection or tender feelings for one another. I was not even confident that they existed. He had seemed uncomfortable with my tentative attempts to engage him more intimately over the years. We did not change in his last days. We talked of trivial things. As before with a dying parent, I did not say goodbye.

Our son came from graduate school in Chicago to visit him. A religiously zealous cousin and his wife arrived and offered Dad a deathbed salvation, which he rejected with some irritation. Dad did not make any last request of me or of Steve, but Dorleen told us that he had told her his wishes for his last rites. He did not want them to be conducted in a church or by a clergyman. He asked that his sons conduct a memorial at the graveside. Since we were staying at his home in Freeport, my brother and I made some plans for the memorial. Steve would conduct the service; I would write and read a eulogy that wove Steve's thoughts together with my own. A new semester was under way at the University of Illinois, so I had to return to Urbana, not knowing how Dad's illness would progress. A few days later on September 17, 1991, he died.

Once more Bonnie and I repeated the trek from Urbana to Freeport, this time to complete funeral arrangements with Steve and Dorleen. I brought my draft of the eulogy with me and read it to Steve. We planned the rest of the graveside service, which was scheduled for eleven in the morning on September 20 in the Greenwood Cemetery in Monroe, where our mother and her parents are also buried.

That morning was cool and brightly sunny, a beautiful day. Our relatives and guests gathered slowly and quietly at the gravesite, where Dad's casket lay over the open grave. The casket was covered with an American flag to honor his service in World War II and his intense love of his country. The spray of fall flowers over the casket was mixed with a golden sheaf of wheat, yellow ears of corn, and corn tassels to honor his life as a farmer. Some chairs were provided under an awning for immediate family members, but most of the company stood. A little wooden lectern was provided for Steve and me. The gathered company and the funeral director watched intently. This was a most unusual funeral ceremony for this conservative rural community: Steve and I conducted the service; there was no clergyman, no religious content except for Steve's reading of Ecclesiastes 3:1–8, which was a tribute to Dad's love of the Bible as literature; no music except for the playing of Taps by a young man who stood on a hill nearby at the close of the ceremony. A squad from the Orangeville chapter of the American Legion folded and presented the flag from the casket to our family (albeit somewhat clumsily, to the annoyance of Steve, who had often participated in such ceremonies as part of a "spit-and-polish" battalion of the Seventh Infantry Division in South Korea).

In my eulogy I reviewed the course of Dad's life, and concluded this way:

It was Steve Switzer's set of values that endures for us today. He was not a religious man in the sense of going to church or praying out loud, but he taught us principles that endure.

He believed that one should be informed about civic and world affairs and that one should be willing to share in the work of self-government. He served on the Orangeville School Board for years, even though milking cows usually made him late for meetings. He brought high standards and a pragmatic approach to the community's problems. He felt that it was a duty to vote— especially to vote Republican.

He believed that one should not seek greater wealth than one's genuine personal needs require. He taught that most of the world's evils result from people seeking unnecessary wealth or power over others.

He taught honesty and rectitude in one's personal dealings.

I don't believe he ever cheated anyone—unless it was himself.

He cherished stewardship of the land and practiced his maxim that one should leave the land better than he found it.

His family grew ever more central in his sense of values. He was proud that his sons married strong, independent women and that their marriages are stable and blessed with mature love. And, oh, how his heart swelled with the love of his three grandchildren, Brian, Stephanie, and Joel, and his pride at the fine young adults they have become.

We do not intend to present a falsely perfect view of our father. He had his faults and came to regret their consequences deeply. From those, living and dead, whom he hurt throughout his life, he sought—as we all must—understanding and forgiveness.

"Do not go gentle into that good night," implored Dylan Thomas of his dying father, "Rage, rage, against the dying of the light." When Dad learned of his cancer late in 1989, he fought his last illness not with rage, but with a brave dignity that eased his passage—not only for him, but also for all of us. Genuinely touched by the sustained outpouring of love and kindness from his family and friends, he gave up some of his old battles with inevitable change and tried to the best of his ability to return the warmth. He learned to take each day as a gift and to take pleasure in the simple acts of life and from those who were close to him. It was a lesson for all to take away: Cherish this day, cherish those whom you love, live as though your time were running out—for it is.

In that context, we confess to our own regret: some peculiar family male reticence inhibited us and our father from speaking openly the simple words of love with one another. Now our deeds must speak for us. These many words are our way of saying the few.

* * * * *

Once the emotions of the day had passed, we turned to the task of settling Dad's estate. Dad had, as he promised, left us a mess. Because they lived near the farm, the bulk of the burden fell to Steve and Dorleen. Steve was appointed executor of the estate in Dad's will. At first, he reacted in anger that no provision had been made to compensate him for the labor that lay ahead, probably honoring a family tradition of convoluting his grief into an emotion that was acceptably displayed by men. Soon, however, we set to work. Both sons and their wives worked together during the days following Dad's death and again during a weekend in October to prepare the contents of the old farmhouse for an auction. We did our work without tears, with almost ruthless efficiency. We discarded perishables and obvious junk, saved important records and family memorabilia, and divided a few items of furniture and many antiques and collectables that we wished to keep. We divided the family "treasures" by collecting them together, tossing a coin to see who chose first, then simply took turns choosing.

Clearly, before the farm could be sold it was necessary to arrange an auction of the contents of the house and farm buildings. Some of Dad's farm equipment was still useful to area farmers, but the auction would primarily attract collectors of old farm equipment and antiques, because so much that my grandparents and parents had collected over the past seventy-five years was still stored on the farm. The auctioneer advised Steve as to optimal ways to display and group the items to be sold. The auction was scheduled for November 9, 1991, and handbills describing it were widely circulated in Illinois, Wisconsin, and Iowa. Late fall was an ideal time for a farm auction, because farmers have usually completed their harvest and look forward to auctions for recreation. The heavy snows of winter were unlikely in early

November, although one could have bad luck if the rains came.

Auctions are a routine feature of rural American life. They serve practical functions, of course, but also as an excuse for social gatherings. In most cases, an odor of loss and failure clings to the proceedings. An auction may be required because, as in the case of our farm, the owner has died or become incapacitated. In many other cases the farmer has surrendered to economic forces and is quitting farming, selling the farm. The most acute psychic pain is inflicted by an auction on farmers who have been forced into bankruptcy. The ritual of a public auction is particularly humiliating to farmers, who tend to be proud and independent.[1] While ours was not a forced sale, this auction was nevertheless a very public demonstration of the demise of the Allison-Switzer farm.

In the days before the auction, Steve and Dorleen and their friends worked hard to clear the buildings and arrange the machinery and old equipment outdoors. They steam-cleaned the tractors and serviced the engines, so they could be started and demonstrated to be in good working order on the day of the auction. They collected many antiques and household items that would be set outdoors. Small items would be arrayed on the wide flat surfaces of hay wagons so that prospective buyers could examine them.

During the ten days prior to the auction Bonnie and I joined a couple of close friends on a long-scheduled trip to France. It would have been understandable if Steve and Dorleen resented the fact that they worked so hard on the preparations for the auction while we enjoyed the wonderful sights, exquisite food, and fine regional wines on a hotel barge on the Burgundy Canal. If so, they didn't speak of it. We flew home on the day before the auction, a long flight that was made even longer by a delay in departing the Paris airport. It was cold and dark when we finally drove from Chicago to Freeport on the day before the auction. On the road from Rockford to Freeport we were startled to see the most spectacular display of the Northern Lights we had ever seen: great streaks of red, yellow, and green lit up the clear black sky. Even the heavens chronicled the passing of an era.

The morning of November 9 was brilliantly sunny, clear, and quite cold—perfect for the auction. Only a little light snow dusted the ground. We drove early to the farm; all was in readiness. The farm machinery, both modern and antique, was arrayed around the barnyard and in a little field south of the buildings. The furniture and household effects were displayed in the yard around the house. How strange and sad to see these familiar objects clustered out on the frozen lawn. There was little for us to do except to guard the small objects against thieves the auctioneer had warned against. Soon pickup trucks and cars filled the field in front of the house, parked all along the lane and along the gravel road at the farm's edge. A crowd of men in seed corn caps and padded jackets and similarly warmly dressed women gathered. The auctioneer began his rhythmic chant and the auction was under way; first the farm machinery, then the household items. The crowd milled about, stamping their feet for warmth, following the auctioneer. A vendor in a little trailer sold food and drinks. Each spectator had items he or she was interested in buying, but for many simply seeing what was for sale and what price it brought was entertainment enough. Our family's junk, the accumulation of seventy-five years, lay scattered about for all to see. By 1991 few remembered Charlie and Mabel Allison, but most had known my mother and father. What were their private thoughts as Stephen and Elva's sons sold off everything on the farm? The antique items brought the greatest interest and the most intense bidding. Many were sold for surprising prices. Even our weathered and gray old outhouse, long separated from the pit below, sold for a hundred dollars.

The day was long and cold. I grew weary of wandering among the wagons and furniture. Somehow I could not summon much interest in the prices these things would bring. By afternoon it became clear that two auctioneers would have to work simultaneously to sell everything by dark. Even so, the light was fading when the last of the household items was sold. The buyers carted their purchases away to their pickup trucks. Even some of the machinery was loaded onto trucks or towed away; the rest would be collected over the next few days.

It was dark when the auctioneer met with us in the warm and brightly lit kitchen to sit at a card table, add up the day's proceeds, collect his percentage and write a check to the estate for the rest. Dorleen had prepared hot food to serve in the barren kitchen and we warmed ourselves with it. The auction had been a great success. Steve and Dorleen were excited by the day's activities and gratified that their efforts had been rewarded.

During the excited talk and the auctioneer's accounting I slipped away and climbed the familiar old steep stairs to the now-empty second floor. I wandered from room to room. How shabby and sad they were when stripped of their furniture. The wallpaper was faded and stained, in some patches completely gone. Ugly rust-colored veins ran along the ceilings and walls. The gray paint on the wooden floors was worn to the bare wood in many places. The boyish wallpaper in my old bedroom spoke to my memory, but the room was now empty, lifeless.

Suddenly, unexpectedly, I found myself crying—not just a few tears, but crying hard, harder than but a few times in my entire adult life. I stumbled from room to room, overcome with grief.

I have wondered since why I wept so. I had not loved the farm. I had yearned to leave it when I was young. My life since leaving the farm had seen the realization of my fondest dreams. Returning to the farm in later years had always provoked ambivalent feelings. I had not wept at my father's death; the tears simply wouldn't come. Now I wept.

I think now that the sight of the empty rooms awakened in me a profound sense of loss: the loss of my grandparents, my mother, my father—all dead now and buried in the cold ground. Was this all that was to come of their lives? These shabby, stained walls? These sad and abandoned rooms? Was this all that came of their years and years of hard work, the cold winters, the hot summers, the illnesses, the hopes and disappointments of two lifetimes? I wept for them.

I wept too for the loss of my youth, the finality of it so baldly laid out before my eyes. I was fifty-one years old now—closer to death than to birth, graying and bald. My children were grown and gone from home. This was the stage on which my young life was played out in all its intensity. Here I lived through the bittersweet experiences of self-discovery, began to dream, to write and create, to feel the young adult emerge. Those days were gone, no less than the farm and all its familiar objects were gone. I wept for myself.

In a few minutes the wave of grief passed. I felt washed clean of the pain and sorrow. I dried my face and composed myself. I slowly descended the steep, worn stairs to the bright rooms below—to a future without the family farm.

The farm house
restored, 2005.

Chapter Seven

Postscript

The farm was sold in 1992 to a farmer who wanted its cultivatable land and had no interest in the buildings, which had stood empty since Dad died. I expected that the big old house would suffer the fate of so many others and fall slowly into ruin, the victim of neglect and decay and perhaps of vandalism. But it was spared. Six acres of land where the house and farm buildings stand were separated and offered for sale in the spring of 1992. Don and Joyce Bates fell in love with the big old house. It had structural problems and was shabby and badly deteriorated inside, but it was large and still had a handsome exterior, and they recognized its potential for restoration. Doing much of the work themselves, they set about renovating and redecorating the house.

The Bates family braced floor joists and added jack posts to shore up the east side of the house. The leaky roof, drafty windows, and ill-fitting doors were replaced. To insulate the house and repair its broken plaster, the interior lath and plaster on the walls and ceilings were removed, insulation was inserted, and covered with dry wall. The result is attractive, but unfortunately nearly all of the original interior woodwork from the 1860s—

wainscotting, doors, doorframes, windows, and window frames—were lost in the process. (A record of those interesting details is preserved, however, in Frank Barmore's appendix to this book.) A roughhewn beam from the barn was added to support a sagging ceiling, adding a rustic touch. Removing walls and adding an upstairs bathroom with a cathedral ceiling and skylight corrected the clumsy arrangement of five upstairs bedrooms that had resulted from the house's history as a two-family house. Floors were leveled and carpeted. Today the entire house has been charmingly restored and is cheerfully, exuberantly, furnished with antiques and country-style decorations.

The Bates did not alter the exterior appearance of the house very much, but they repainted it and trimmed it in bright red. The badly deteriorated old scale house, garage, and chicken house were removed. The remaining buildings were repainted in traditional red barn paint. Repairs were made to the south windows of the barn, but otherwise it has not been altered. A large green lawn, flowerbeds, and a mixture of young trees and landscaping that survives from decades ago surround the entire cluster of buildings. Thanks to their love of old farm buildings, the Bates have rescued the 145-year-old structures from decay and ruin and assured their survival for many years to come.

167   Postscript

Notes

Prologue

1   R. Douglas Hurt, *American Agriculture: A Brief History*, 396.

2   B. F. Stanton, "Changes in Farm Size and Structure in American Agriculture in the Twentieth Century," 42–70.

3   Stanton, "Changes in Farm Size and Structure," 44.

4   Ibid., 50.

5   Hurt, *American Agriculture*, 242.

6   Ibid., 395.

Chapter One

1   R. Douglas Hurt, *American Agriculture: A Brief History*, 221.

2   U. S. Department of Agriculture, *Annual Report,* 1911, 650.

3   Hurt, *American Agriculture*, 396.

4   U. S. Department of Agriculture, *Annual Report,* 1911, 651.

5   During the first four decades of the twentieth century tenant farmers operated between 30 and 40 percent of all U.S. farms; by 1987 only about one in ten farms were operated by renters. B. F. Stanton, "Changes in Farm Size and Structure in American Agriculture in the Twentieth Century," 59.

6   In the Annual Report of the U. S. Department of Agriculture in 1920, the Secretary of Agriculture stated that "the average price per acre of land and improvements in 1920 is two and one-half times that of 1910 and five times that of twenty years ago," and went on to comment, "if he [a farmer] borrows a considerable part of the purchase price of a farm at from 5 to 7 percent and then finds that the investment will earn little more than 3 percent, it will be impossible, in many instances, for him to discharge the debt." This dry summary described Charlie and Mabel's situation quite accurately. According to Dennis S. Nordin and Roy V. Scott in *From Prairie Farmer to Entrepreneur: The Transformation of Midwestern Agriculture* (25), the price per acre paid by Charlie and Mabel was within normal ranges for the period; Illinois farmland averaged $108 per acre in 1910, but rose to an average of $188 per acre in 1920.

7   David B. Danbom, *Born in the County: A History of Rural America*, 220–23.

8   U. S. Department of Agriculture. *A Brief History of the Rural Electrification and Telephone Program.* The situation was slightly better in the Midwest. In 1920, 9.8 percent of Illinois farms had electricity, but this had increased to only 16 percent by 1930 (Dennis S. Nordin and Roy V. Scott, *From Prairie Farmer to Entrepreneur*, 65.)

9   Robert F. Ensminger, *The Pennsylvania Barn. Its Origin, Evolution and Distribution in North America.* Although old barns continue to disappear rapidly from the American rural landscape, there exists great fascination for these

evocative old structures and a movement for their preservation and restoration (for example, see the website for Barn Again, www.agriculture.com/barnagain). Hundreds of books and articles have been written about old barns; many are beautifully illustrated. Ensminger's book provides the best description of the style of barn built in the 1860s on the Allison-Switzer (then the Barmore) farm, which is classified as an open (or posted) fore-bay standard Pennsylvania frame bank barn. Example B on p. 124 is quite close to the structural design of the original barn. Many standard Pennsylvania barns were built of stone or with stone sidewalls, but the Midwestern versions were entirely of wood frame construction. Also, see the appendix to this book by Frank E. Barmore for a detailed description of the architecture of the barn.

10 I have based my reconstruction of my grandparents' lives in this chapter on many of their and my parents' oral accounts, on my direct experience of the way we farmed in the years from 1946 to 1949 before significant modernization of the farm, from youthful observations of other old-fashioned farmers, from my knowledge of the use of antique farm implements found on the farm and elsewhere and from exhibitions of antique farm equipment in which it was shown in operation.

11 Readers who would like to see illustrations of the horse-powered machinery and other agricultural equipment described in this book will find the following reference valuable: Robert K. Mills (ed.), *Implement & Tractor: Reflections on 100 Years of Farm Equipment*. Based largely on illustrated advertisements from the trade journal Implement & Tractor, this volume contains many fine drawings of virtually all of the farm implements described in chapters 2, 3, and 4. The illustrations of horse-drawn machinery are especially useful for readers who are unfamiliar with the equipment used by Charlie and Mabel Allison from 1916 to 1946. Examples include a manure spreader, p. 118; plows, pp. 16, 55; harrows and discs, pp. 18, 57, 96; grain drill, pp. 52, 82; corn planter, pp. 42, 96; corn cultivator, pp. 12, 112; hay mower, pp. 50, 77; hay dump rake, pp. 65, 77; hay loader, pp. 51, 96; farm wagon, p. 49; grain binder, p. 50. Many examples of threshers, steam engines, early tractors and gasoline engines, and household appliances are also shown. Also valuable is Ronald Stokes Barlow, *Three Hundred Years of Farm Implements and Machinery: 1630–1930*. This book is lavishly illustrated with large, detailed figures, some in color, from contemporary advertising and trade literature depicting all of the farm equipment described in chapters 2, 3, and 4. It is especially strong in its descriptions of horse-powered machinery and early steam- and gasoline-powered equipment. Items depicted of particular interest to readers of chapter 2 include: harvesting loose hay with as harpoon fork and pulley system (pp. 80–81), a hand-operated corner planter used by Charlie (p. 44, third from left), a husking pin used for harvesting corn by hand (p. 75, left), singletrees and double trees used to hitch teams of horse to wagons and machinery (p. 166), gasoline engines of the type used by Charlie to pump water when there was too little wind to power the windmill (p. 131), and much more.

12 Hurt, *American Agriculture*, 244.

13 Ibid., 230.

14 The University of Illinois's Morrow Plots are an early and outstanding example. For a good brief history of the plots see Crop Sciences Research and Education Center, "The Morrow Plots: A Century of Learning."

15 Mark Friedberger, *Farm Families and Change in Twentieth-Century America*, 18.

16 Ibid.

17 Hurt, *American Agriculture*, 252–56.

18 Friedberger, *Farm Families and Change in Twentieth-Century America*, 18.

19 A beautifully detailed description of domestic life in rural America in the 1930s that parallels the lives of the Allison family from 1916 to 1940 is found in Mildred Armstrong Kalish, *Little Heathens: Hard Times and High Spirits on an Iowa Farm During the Great Depression*.

20 News reports may be found in the June 22 and June 24, 1944 issues of the *Dixon Evening Telegraph* (Illinois).

21 James H. Shideler, *Farm Crisis, 1919-1923*, 46.

22 Nordin and Scott, *From Prairie Farmer to Entrepreneur*, 53.

23 U.S. Department of Agriculture, *Yearbook of Agriculture, 1931*, 32.

24 Ibid.

25 U.S. Department of Agriculture, *Agricultural Statistics, 1936*, 354.

26 Danbom, *Born in the Country*, 199.

27 Ibid., 231.

28 Hurt, *American Agriculture*, 321. Wylie D. Goodsell, Ronald W. Jones, and Russell W. Bierman, *Typical Family-Operated Farms, 1930-45: Adjustments, Costs and Returns*, 34–7 presents a detailed description of the economics of typical mixed dairy-hog-poultry farms in southern Wisconsin very much like Charlie and Mabel's farm through the Depression and World War II years. Net income on farms of this type averaged about $540 annually from 1931 through 1934, rose modestly to $1,400 per year from 1935 through 1939, but had jumped to $4,600 by 1944 and 1945. Of course, expenses rose in the war years too, but not so steeply as farm prices. This reference provides detailed economic data for many other types of family-operated farms during this period.

29 Friedberger, *Farm Families and Change in Twentieth-Century America*, 17–8.

30 Urias J. Hoffman and William S. Booth, *The One-Room and Consolidated Country Schools of Illinois*. This report contains fascinating detailed standards for one-room schools of the period and documents progress toward upgrading Illinois schools to meet these standards.

31 Ibid., 22–4.

32 Burton W. Kreitlow, *Rural Education: Community Backgrounds*, 22.

33 Ibid., 24.

34 Readers who wish to learn more about Carthage College during the years Elva attended may consult Harold H. Lentz, *The Miracle of Carthage. History of Carthage College, 1847-1974*. The Carthage Public Library (538 Wabash, Carthage, Ill.) has a collection of Carthage College yearbooks, including the years from 1926 through 1931, which give a good picture of college life at that time. Much about Elva's favorite biology professor Prof. Alice L. Kibbe and her many contributions to Carthage College and the Carthage community can be learned by visiting the Kibbe-Hancock Museum, also located in Carthage.

Chapter Two

1 A large literature documents that Dad was generally correct in this view.

To provide a simple snapshot, Mark Friedberger in *Farm Families and Change in Twentieth-Century America*, 54, tabulated farm mortgage foreclosures in a group of thirty-one Iowa counties from 1915 through 1936. Foreclosures averaged 67 per year from 1915–1920, rose sharply to 607 per year from 1921–1929, peaked at an average of 1,313 per year from 1930–1932 and remained at 640 per year from 1933–1936. Overall, almost 20 percent of the total farm acreage in the survey area was involved in foreclosures from 1915–1936. 1937 was a drought year, which compounded the misery.

2   U.S. Department of Agriculture, *Agricultural Statistics*, 1950, 560.

3   Three common forms of dairy farming were found in the first decades of the twentieth century. Farms located near cities and larger towns sold fresh milk to be bottled for human consumption because it could be transported to the diaries without spoiling. In more remote areas two other patterns dominated. In the northern Midwest cheese makers—often Swiss, German, or Italian immigrants—set up small factories near dairy farms and sold cheese and cream. Charlie and Mabel Allison (chapter 2) and later my parents (chapters 4 and 5) sold their milk to such a rural cheese factory. Here, my father describes the third common pattern: The farmer kept a relatively small dairy herd, and the family used a portion of the milk. From the excess milk the farmer sold the cream and fed the skim milk to hogs. This was apparently also the pattern followed by the Barmore family in the years prior to 1911.

4   Wayne E. Fuller, *One-Room Schools in the Middle West: An Illustrated History*, 109.

5   Urias J. Hoffman and William S. Booth, *The One-Room and Consolidated Country Schools of Illinois* had specified a minimum salary for teachers in rural one-room schools of $40 a month seventeen years earlier.

6   R. Douglas Hurt, *American Agriculture: A Brief History*, 292; David B. Danbom, *Born in the County: A History of Rural America*, 209–10.

Chapter Three

1   The Allison farm was more advanced than average in this respect. By 1947, 60 percent of farms had electrical service, but only 34 percent had telephones. In 1949 the Rural Electrification Administration was authorized to support the installation of rural telephone systems, as it had supported rural electrification since 1936. See U.S. Department of Agriculture, *A Brief History of the Rural Electric and Telephone Program*.

2   The number of farm tractors in the United States soared in the postwar period from 1.55 million in 1940 to 3.83 million in 1950. Sales of tractors were 25,000 per year in 1932–33, but climbed to more than 500,000 per year in 1949–50. U.S. Department of Agriculture, *Agricultural Statistics*, 1950, 574.

3   As an example, a farmer could plow an acre in thirty minutes with a tractor, whereas it would have taken him 1.8 hours with a horse-drawn plow. David B. Danbom, *Born in the Country: A History of Rural America*, 317.

4   Burton W. Kreitlow, *Rural Education: Community Backgrounds*, 252–8 provides a good description of the On-Farm Training program and an evaluation of its effectiveness.

5   Ernest Thompson Robbins, *Cheaper and more profitable pork thru swine sanitation: a review of the McLean County system of swine sanitation on Illinois farms*

during 1925.

6   Dennis S. Nordin and Roy V. Scott, *From Prairie Farmer to Entrepreneur: The Transformation of Midwestern Agriculture*, 140.

7   R. Douglas Hurt, *Problems of Plenty: The American Farmer in the Twentieth Century*, 97–123.

8   R. Douglas Hurt, *American Agriculture: A Brief History*, 325, 395.

9   Ibid., 395.

10   In 1966, wives and other family members contributed from 22 to 28 percent of the total hours of labor on Midwestern farms (Nordin and Scott, *From Prairie Farmer to Entrepreneur*, 163). This percentage was probably even higher in earlier years when farms were less mechanized.

11   David E. Lindstrom, *Development of Rural Community Schools in Illinois*. This source provides a detailed description of political and sociological factors involved in rural school consolidation in Illinois from 1920 to 1957. See also Wayne E. Fuller, *One-Room Schools in the Middle West: An Illustrated History*, 119. Interestingly, Wisconsin was much slower than Illinois to abandon its one-room schools; of 6,600 in use in 1932, 3,700 were still operating in 1954.

Chapter Four

1   B. F. Stanton, "Changes in Farm Size and Structure in American Agriculture in the Twentieth Century," 44.

2   Early in the twentieth century most dairy states passed laws governing sanitation of milk sold for human consumption. Such laws generally provided for two standards: producers of Grade A milk, which could be sold directly as fluid milk, were required to meet higher sanitation standards than were farmers selling Grade B milk, which could be used for nonfluid manufacturing purposes such as cheese, butter, nonfat dry milk, and ice cream. Standards for both grades were raised over the years by revisions in state laws. Regular testing of milk for bacterial contamination, testing of cows for tuberculosis, and inspection of barns and milk storage facilities for construction standards and cleanliness were required. Illinois law detailing the standards for farms producing Grade A milk in 1950 are described in Illinois Department of Health, *Grade A Milk Law*. An example of the extensive renovations required for upgrading barns and milk houses to meet Grade A standards in the 1950s is given in C. J., Fentzau and R. N. Van Arsdall, *Meeting Dairy Market Sanitation Requirements Economically: A Preliminary Report*. Although Dad's barn and milk storage did not meet Grade A standards, the Grade B milk sold by my family was regularly tested at the cheese factory for bacterial contamination by a methylene blue test and for sediment and dirt by filtration. The barn was occasionally inspected by public health workers. Dad's cattle were vaccinated for brucellosis (undulant fever in humans) and tested for tuberculosis. The milk was pasteurized at the cheese factory before use (although we and other farm families drank their own milk without pasteurizing it). By the end of the twentieth century, virtually all milk producers met Grade A standards and Grade B milk was no longer produced.

3   Mark Friedberger, *Farm Families and Change in Twentieth-Century America*, 127–42 presents a thoughtful analysis of farm families who successfully enlarged their holdings, illustrating his generalizations with descriptions of specific farm families. Strong family loyalties, great discipline and hard work, often directed

by a patriarch, and considerable financial acumen were the keys to building family farm "empires."

4   This kind of "intervivos" or pre-death transfer of farms to family members was practiced by about one-fifth of Midwest farmers according to Friedberger, *Farm Families and Change in Twentieth-Century America*, 78–83.

5   Richard F. Fallert, *Dairy: Background for 1985 Legislation: Agriculture Information Bulletin.*

6   Even though the number of diary cows and commercial dairy farms in the United States dropped by more than two-thirds from 1959 to 1983, the high prices in the late 1970s and early 1980s led to large surpluses. The cost of the federal dairy price support program ballooned to $2.6 billion in the 1982–83 production year. (See Fallert, *Dairy*, 15, 27, 38).

Chapter Five

1   R. Douglas Hurt, *American Agriculture: A Brief History*, 395.

2   Carolyn Dimitri, Anne Effland, and Neilson Conklin, *The 20th Century Transformation of U.S. Agriculture and Farm Policy.*

3   R. Douglas Hurt, *Problems of Plenty: The American Farmer in the Twentieth Century*, 124–53; David B. Danbom, *Born in the County: A History of Rural America*, 233–57.

4   The economic factors leading to this crisis have been thoroughly and skillfully analyzed by Neil E. Harl in *The Farm Debt Crisis of the 1980s* and Barry J. Barnett in "The U.S. Farm Financial Crisis of the 1980s," 160–71. The human and sociological impact of the crisis is movingly presented by Kathryn Marie Dudley, *Debt and Dispossession: Farm Loss in America's Heartland.*

5   Barnett, "The U.S. Farm Financial Crisis of the 1980s," 165.

6   Harl, *The Farm Debt Crisis of the 1980s*, 39.

7   Ibid., 3–17.

8   Ibid., 39.

9   Ibid., 32.

10   Ibid., 20.

11   This rather harshly judgmental view of farmers who were overwhelmed by debt was quite common according to Harl in *The Farm Debt Crisis of the 1980s*, 39–41 and Dudley, *Debt and Dispossession*, 105–23.

Chapter Six

1   Kathryn M. Dudley, *Debt and Dispossession*, 126-131 vividly describes the painful reactions of farmers forced into bankruptcy during the 1980s to the auction of their farm equipment.

Image Gallery: Chapters 1-3

Charlie and Mabel Allison's wedding certificate, February 15, 1906.

Charlie and Mabel Allison at the time of their marriage in 1906.

Four generations of mothers, 1907: Susan (Hackworth) Whitehead (Delila's mother), above; Delila Campbell (Mabel's mother), left; Mabel Allison (Elva's mother), right; Elva Allison (my mother), below.

Elva on her grandparent's farm
around 1910. (bottom) Charlie Allison
in typical farm clothing, 1944.

Elva Allison (left) and Steve Switzer (right) at high school graduation in 1925 and 1929, respectively.

(left) Steve and Elva in their courtship years, 1932. (right) Steve, our father, home on leave from the Navy with my brother, then called Allison, left, and me on the Allison farm in 1944.

(top) Interior of Pleasant Hill School in January 1947. I am a first-grader seated second from the front of the photo in the left row. My brother is seated second from the front in the right row. (bottom) Pleasant Hill School on the southwest corner of the farm in 1919.

I am the farm boy with pigs in about
1950 (top) and 1957 (bottom).

The top photo of the farmhouse was taken in 1944, but the house was little changed thirty-three years later (bottom).

(top) Charlie and Mabel, my grandparents, in about 1950. (bottom)
Charlie Allison in 1962. *Rockford
Register Star*/Copyrighted/Used
with permission.

Image Gallery: Chapters 4-7

Steve Switzer with his grandchildren
on the Frank Switzer farm in 1981;
from left: Steve, Brian, Joel, Stephanie.

Brian and Stephanie at play on their Grandpa Switzer's farm, 1978.

The Switzer farm in 1977.

Making hay on Grandpa Switzer's farm, 1979.

Winter moods on the farm.

The Farm in decay. Photographs
by Brian Switzer, 1987.

Grandpa Switzer with his farm cats.
Photographs by Stephanie Switzer, 1990.

Flyer announcing the Switzer
farm auction in 1991 (complete with
misspelling of "HUGE").

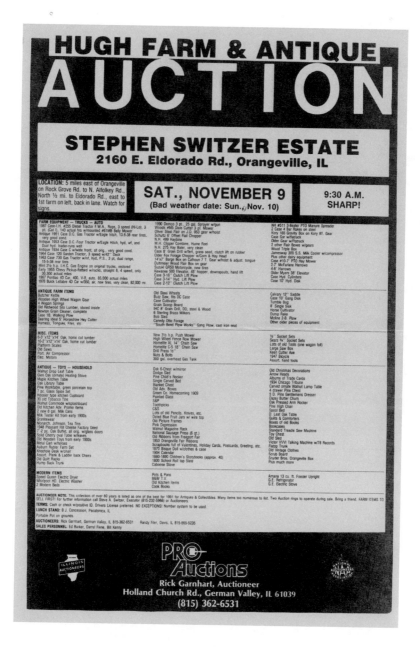

Scenes from the farm auction,
November 9, 1991.

The abandoned farmhouse after
the auction, 1991.

(top and bottom left) The farm buildings restored, 2005. (bottom right) Interior of the haymow in the old barn. The photo was taken in 2005, but the structure of the barn is essentially the same as when it was built in about 1867.

Image Gallery: The Farm in Art

Switzer Barn.
Watercolor by Bonnie Switzer.

Cornstalk.
Watercolor by Bonnie Switzer.

Gingerbread Porch.
Watercolor by Bonnie Switzer.

Switzer Farm Remembered.
Watercolor by Bonnie Switzer.

Farm Cats.
Woodblock print by Brian Switzer.

Pleasant Hill School.
Woodblock print by Brian Switzer.

Grandpa Contemplates the Future.
Woodblock print by Brian Switzer.

Abandoned Horse-drawn Haymower.
Woodblock print by Brian Switzer.

Bibliography

Barlow, Ronald Stokes, *Three Hundred Years of Farm Implements and Machinery: 1630–1930* (Iola, Wisc.: Krause Publications, 2003).

Barnett, Barry J., "The U.S. Farm Financial Crisis of the 1980s," in Jane Adams (ed.), *Fighting for the Farm: Rural America Transformed* (Philadelphia: University of Pennsylvania Press, 2003).

Crop Sciences Research and Education Center, University of Illinois, "The Morrow Plots: A Century of Learning." Available at www.cropsci.uiuc.edu/research/rdc/urbana/morrow.cfm, last accessed June 23, 2008.

Danbom, David B., *Born in the County: A History of Rural America*, 2nd ed. (Baltimore: Johns Hopkins University Press, 2006). A good general history of American agriculture from pre-colonial to modern times.

Dimitri, Carolyn, Anne Effland, and Neilson Conklin, *The 20th Century Transformation of U.S. Agriculture and Farm Policy*, Economic Information Bulletin No. 3 (Washington, D.C.: U.S. Department of Agriculture, 2005).

Dudley, Kathryn Marie, *Debt and Dispossession: Farm Loss in America's Heartland* (Chicago: University of Chicago Press, 2000). Farm bankruptcies reached a peak during the 1920s and 1930s, but another wave of financial crises swept America's farmers in the 1980s. This well written and deeply felt book describes the experiences of a community of Minnesota farm families who lost or nearly lost their farms and the reactions of the surrounding community. The economic conditions that led to their crises are clarified, and the personal costs to their families are movingly described, often in the farmers' own words. The author has a deep understanding of the psychology and sociology of midwestern farmers.

Ensminger, Robert F., *The Pennsylvania Barn: Its Origin, Evolution and Distribution in North America* (Baltimore: Johns Hopkins University Press, 1992).

Fallert, Richard F., "Dairy: Background for 1985 Legislation," *Agriculture Information Bulletin*, No. 474 (Washington, D.C.: U.S. Department of Agriculture, Economic Research Service, 1985).

Fentzau, C. J., and R. N. Arsdall, *Meeting Dairy Market Sanitation Requirements Economically: A Preliminary Report*, Marketing Research Report No. 64 (Washington, D.C.: U.S. Department of Agriculture, 1954).

Friedberger, Mark, *Farm Families and Change in Twentieth-Century America* (Lexington: University Press of Kentucky, 1988). A valuable sociological study of farm families, the author presents case studies from two types of farms: traditional Iowa corn belt farms like that described in this book, and, in contrast, commodity farms in California's central valley.

Fuller, Wayne E., *One-Room Schools in the Middle West: An Illustrated History* (Lawrence: University of Kansas Press, 1994). Chapters 9–11 provide a good background, with many photographs, for readers interested in one-room country schools like Pleasant Hill Dist. No. 4 attended by my mother from 1916 to 1921 and my brother and me from 1946 to 1952.

Goodsell, Wylie D., Ronald W. Jones, and Russell W. Bierman, *Typical Family-Operated Farms, 1930–45: Adjustments, Costs and Returns* (Washington, D.C.: U.S. Department of Agriculture, Bureau of Agricultural Economics, 1948).

Hallam, Arne (ed.), *Size, Structure and the Changing Face of American Agriculture* (Boulder, Colo.: Westview Press, 1993). This volume presents a collection of articles containing a wealth of statistical data concerning changes in farm economics during the twentieth century.

Harl, Neil E., *The Farm Debt Crisis of the 1980s* (Ames: Iowa State University Press, 1990).

Hoffman, Urias J., and William S. Booth, *The One-Room and Consolidated Country Schools of Illinois* (Springfield: Superintendent of Public Instruction Circular 124, Sixth Edition, 1917).

Hurt, R. Douglas, *American Agriculture: A Brief History* (Ames: Iowa State University Press, 1994). Intended for the general reader, this book traces the history of farming from the agriculture of Native Americans before colonization to the mechanized mass farming of today.

Hurt, R. Douglas, *Problems of Plenty: The American Farmer in the Twentieth Century* (Chicago: Ivan R. Dee, 2002).

Illinois Department of Public Health, *Grade A Milk Law*, Circular 135 (Springfield: Illinois Department of Public Health, 1950).

Jager, Ronald, *The Fate of Family Farming: Variations on an American Idea* (Lebanon, N.H.: University Press of New England, 2004). Jager's book examines the past and future of family farming from a historical-philosophical perspective and emphasizes family farming in New England, although most of his generalizations apply to American farming elsewhere. He provides an overview of the writings of what I call "philosopher-farmers," who view agrarianism and family farming poetically and idealistically—and sometimes with alarm. The book gives examples of family farms in New Hampshire that are thriving and suggests the ways in which small family farms will survive in the future.

Kalish, Mildred Armstrong, *Little Heathens: Hard Times and High Spirits on an Iowa Farm During the Great Depression* (New York: Bantam Books, 2002). This charming book provides a rich portrait of growing up on an Iowa farm during the Depression and is laced with humor and insight. It is particularly interesting for its presentation of the daily lives of rural women and girls in the 1930s.

Koop, Frederic B., *The Good Life: An Intimate Portrait of Life on the Farms of America* (Cincinnati: F & W Publishing, 1961). A detailed, if rather sentimental, portrait with many photographs of American farm life in the 1950s.

Kreitlow, Burton W., *Rural Education: Community Backgrounds* (New York: Harper and Brothers, 1954).

Lentz, Harold H., *The Miracle of Carthage: History of Carthage College, 1847–1974* (Lima, Ohio: C.S.S. Publishing Co., 1975).

Lieberman, Archie, *Farm Boy* (New York: Abrams, 1974). A book of photographs depicting the everyday life of a teenage farm boy in northwestern Illinois. These photographs are evocative of the settings in which my brother and I grew up on the Orangeville farm, and provide a visual tapestry of our lives during the 1950s.

Lindstrom, David E., *Development of Rural Community Schools in Illinois*, Bulletin 627 (Urbana: University of Illinois, Agricultural Experiment Station, 1958).

Meyer, Carrie A., *Days on the Family Farm: From the Golden Age Through the Great Depression* (Minneapolis: University of Minnesota Press, 2007). This very detailed description of life on a farm in northern Illinois from 1900 to 1944 is based on a collection of dairies and fiscal ledgers kept by the author's family members. These sources are interwoven with thorough research into the economic and social history of period.

Mills, Robert K. (ed.), *Implement & Tractor: Reflections on 100 Years of Farm Equipment* (Overland Park, Kans.: Intertec Publishing Corp., 1986).

Nordin, Dennis S., and Roy V. Scott, *From Prairie Farmer to Entrepreneur: The Transformation of Midwestern Agriculture* (Bloomington: Indiana University Press, 2005). This history of economic, technological, and social changes in American agriculture during the twentieth century is very thoroughly researched and presents richly detailed documentary data.

Robbins, Ernest Thompson, *Cheaper and more profitable pork thru swine sanitation: a review of the McLean County system of swine sanitation on Illinois farms during 1925*, Circular 306 (Urbana: University of Illinois, Agricultural College and Experiment Station, 1926).

Rosenblatt, Paul C., *Farming is in Our Blood: Farm Families in Economic Crisis* (Ames: Iowa State University Press, 1990). Like the book by Kathryn Dudley, this work presents an intimate portrait of the human side of the farm crisis of the 1980s through interviews with affected families. Though focused on a group of farmers in Minnesota during the 1980s, many of their attitudes and experiences represent American farmers in general.

Shideler, James H., *Farm Crisis, 1919–1923* (Berkeley: University of California Press, 1957).

Stanton, B. F., "Changes in Farm Size and Structure in American Agriculture in the Twentieth Century, in Arne Hallam, ed., *Size, Structure and the Changing Face of American Agriculture* (Boulder, Colo: Westview Press, 1993).

U.S. Department of Agriculture, *Agricultural Statistics*, 1936, 1950 (Washington, D.C.: U.S. Government Printing Office).

U.S. Department of Agriculture, *Annual Report*, 1911 (Washington, D.C.: U.S. Government Printing Office.

U.S. Department of Agriculture, "Rural Electrification Administration. A Brief History of the Rural Electric and Telephone Programs," (1984). Available at www.rurdev.usda.gov/rd/70th/rea-history.pdf.

U.S. Department of Agriculture, *Yearbook of Agriculture*, 1931 (Washington, D.C.: U.S. Government Printing Office).

Appendix
The Barmore Family Farm
Stephenson County, Illinois

A Note on the Appendix

By chance I was visiting my father on our family farm some time in the 1970s when Frank Barmore first visited his ancestral family farm. It was the only time we have met in person. Frank introduced himself and explained that he was a descendant of Nathaniel J. Barmore, who had lived on the farm for many years and built the house and barn that still stood before us. He was a grandson of Benjamin B. Barmore, whose name we had often heard as "Uncle Ben" from our neighbors, Glenn Barmore and Jennings Cahoon, who were grandsons of N. J. Barmore. Frank was interested in tracing his family's history and especially keen to examine the architectural details of the old house and barn. Dad shared with him as much information as he had, and then we left him to his work. He carefully and thoroughly examined the old house, taking measurements, making drawings, and tracing the details of the woodwork, windows, and doorframes. He returned some time later to examine the old barn with equal care.

In 1978, Frank sent my father a copy of a beautifully handwritten description of the old farm house complete with many drawings and details. This document was the first draft of a major section of the appendix that follows. I don't think Frank was particularly concerned with publication of his work; his objective was to preserve his family's rich history. I saved a copy of Frank's document, but gave it little thought until I had completed the first draft of this manuscript some thirty years later. It was clear to me that Frank's material would make a fine supplement to my memoir, but I had had no contact with him for many years and had no idea where he was. Thanks to the power of the Internet, I was able to locate Frank in LaCrosse, Wisconsin, and learned that he was, like me, a retired professor. I proposed that he submit his descriptions of the old farm house as an appendix to my book, and to my delight he not only agreed, but offered to expand the work to include some background material on the history of the Barmore family and the farm from 1858 to 1911 when they lived there and his descriptions and drawings of the old barn. The editors at the Center for American Places enthusiastically agreed with our plan as soon as they saw my copy of Frank's 1978 document.

Frank and I have not met in person again, but through our e-mail and telephone conversations, I feel I have come to know him a little. He is a man of few words, a very thorough and precise scholar, and an excellent draftsman. Thanks to his carefully detailed appendix, the story of my family farm has been extended back by more than fifty years to include the story of his family farm, essentially tracing its history back to the time when the land was first transferred by the U.S. government to the first grantees, the Starr family, in the 1840s. For Frank Barmore, as for me, this story of "our" family farm has been a labor of love.

Robert L. Switzer
September 2008

The Barmore Family Farm, Stephenson County, Illinois
by Frank E. Barmore

I. The Family

Nathaniel Jennings Barmore was born on February 11, 1828 in Greene County, Pennsylvania, the second son and the fifth of seven children of Joseph Barmore (1792 NJ–1874 WI) and his first wife, Salome Jennings (1797 PA–1862 WI). Joseph and his family moved to Ohio in 1841 and then to Wisconsin in 1848–49. In the 1850 Federal Census the family, save the eldest son, Alfred, is farming, but not owning, 320 acres of improved and unimproved land in Clarno Township, Green County, Wisconsin. Alfred is farming nearby, close to Twin Grove in Jefferson Township, also in Green County.

On December 9, 1851, Nathaniel married Susanna Stair (1831 IN–1921 CA), the daughter of Jacob Stair and Elizabeth Fluke, in the house of his brother, Alfred, near Twin Grove. They lived for a year in a spring house converted to a cabin, a mile east of Twin Grove, and their first child, Salome Elizabeth, was born there in September of 1852. Within a year, Nathaniel moved south across the state line into Stephenson County, Illinois, where he remained. Joseph had also moved to Stephenson County, but in March 1853 he purchased farmland in Jefferson Township Green County, Wisconsin and returned to Wisconsin where he lived for the rest of his life. It is as if Nathaniel traded places with his father, Joseph. Did he?

Nathaniel must have been a successful farmer. He was able to generate the cash necessary to purchase his own farm and, over the following decades, substantial additional land (see Section II). He was able to raise a family of nine children (see the chart of the children and grandchildren). He had the resources to build the house and barn that are still on the farm and still in use (see sections III and IV). He lived to see the surviving seven children married and settled on their own farms. The exact nature and magnitude of the financial help that he received from his father,

Joseph, and that he was able to give his children is unknown, but the various land transfers are very suggestive.

See the works by Frank E. Barmore, Ruth A. Barmore, and William H. Jennings for additional information about the Barmore family. Throughout this appendix sources referred to parenthetically will be found in the reference list at the end of the appendix.

II. The Farm

It is not known exactly where Nathaniel lived and farmed during the years 1853–58, but the children born in these years were born in Rock Grove Township in Stephenson County, so it is possible, but not demonstrated, that they could have been on the land that Nathaniel purchased in 1858 from the Starr family. The Starr family had purchased at least 880 acres of public land in the area—perhaps more than they could exploit by themselves except by renting it out or selling it.

In 1858 Nathaniel purchased 120 acres: the SW-¼ and the E-½ of the NW-¼ of Sec 27, T29N, R8E, 4th Principle Meridian. There were also twenty acres of timberland nearby in Wisconsin that he had acquired in the 1850s. The original survey plats are available (see Government Land Office records.) They show that the purchased land in Illinois was part of a large prairie, miles across, with timberland beginning two miles to the east and a mile to the northwest. The timberland to the northwest continued well into Wisconsin and included the timberland that Nathaniel owned there. Detailed notes by the original surveyors indicate that the timber consisted of sugar maple, basswood, red oak, white oak, and black oak (see Finley). One wonders if this timber was the source of the oak beams in the house and barn that were built later.

A Stephenson County plat map dated 1859 (see Dunham) shows the 120 acres that Nathaniel owned at that time. That map shows a dwelling in the center of the SE 40 acres of the 120 acres owned by Nathaniel. The location of the dwelling is well removed from the locations of later dwellings on the 120 acres. Perhaps the family lived there until 1867 (Refer to the Map and Table I, Land Transactions).

In 1867 a substantial house was built. Jennie Jennings Barmore has related that she was the first child born in the house, it being completed during the summer a few months prior to her birth in

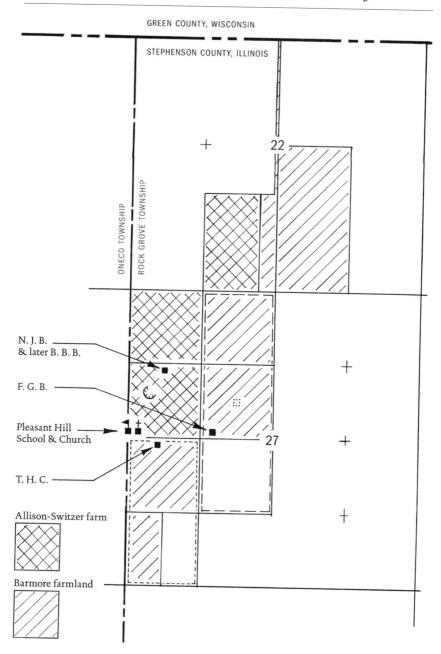

GREEN COUNTY, WISCONSIN

STEPHENSON COUNTY, ILLINOIS

ONECO TOWNSHIP

ROCK GROVE TOWNSHIP

22

N. J. B.
& later B. B. B.

F. G. B.

Pleasant Hill
School & Church

27

T. H. C.

Allison-Switzer farm

Barmore farmland

November 1867. The barn was built about the same time and is located approximately two hundred feet to the west. Nathaniel's father, Joseph (then seventy-four, widowed and remarried) sold the last major parcel of his farmland in Wisconsin in November of 1866 and moved into the city of Monroe, Wisconsin in March of 1867. Was there a transfer of resources to Nathaniel? Or perhaps the resources to build the house and barn were the result of strong prices and demand for farm products during the Civil War (1861–1865).

In the nineteenth century the production of the farm is well described by the Productions of Agriculture schedules in the decennial Federal Census returns. Those for 1860, 1870, and 1880 are summarized in Table II. Some of the trends are typical of the region and the era. Wheat production declined while corn, oats, and hay increased. Milk production increased, but not for sale or cheese. Given the numbers, it would seem it was either used by the family or separated with the cream becoming butter and the skim milk fed to the hogs and cattle.

In 1874, Nathaniel purchased sixty acres south of and adjacent to his farm. This brought Nathaniel's holdings to 261 acres of "developed" farmland in Rock Grove Township. And there were also twenty acres of timberland nearby in Wisconsin. Though there were later additional acquisitions, the trend in the future would be toward establishing his children on farms of their own.

Nathaniel's oldest son, Frank, married in 1879 and began farming by renting land from his father for a share of the production. In 1892 Nathaniel sold eighty acres to Frank and this became the core of Frank's 120-acre farm adjacent to and east of Nathaniel. Also in 1892, Nathaniel and his two sons, Jacob and Benjamin, purchased 240 acres $1\frac{1}{2}$ miles to the sw in Oneco Township. Two-thirds or 160 acres of this became the farm of Jacob, who married in January of 1893. Nathaniel retained the remaining eighty acres, and his estate sold it to persons outside the family.

Mary married Benjamin F. Chambers in 1878 and they had a farm $2\frac{3}{4}$ miles away to the ENE. Jennie married Harrison L. Raymer in December 1892, and they had a farm 12/3 miles away to the NNE, on the state line in Wisconsin. Benjamin married in December of 1893 and began farming the 121 acres, which he later purchased from his father in 1903. Ruth Anna married John F. Gift in January 1895 and they had a farm $1\frac{1}{10}$ mile to the NW in Oneco Township.

With all the children married and Benjamin farming much, if not all, of the remaining land, Nathaniel, now almost sixty-seven, retired from active farming. He built a one-story addition on the east end of the house containing a kitchen, pantry, and summer kitchen and moved into these retirement accommodations—the expanded east portion of the house. Benjamin and his growing family occupied the west portion of the house. About the time that Benjamin purchased the farm (1903), the eastern extension of the house was detached and moved south about a quarter-mile up the hill and attached to the house of his widowed daughter, Salome (Barmore) Cahoon. Nathaniel and Susanna remained there until Nathaniel died December 15, 1911.

Some insight into the evolution of the farm under Benjamin's tenure is gained from the reminiscences of his son, John Jennings Barmore, a half-century later.

The hay fields and pastures were all domesticated varieties as no prairie grass remained. Other crops were corn, oats, and barley. Some were sold, the remainder used on the farm. They always had hogs: "They were where the money came from." The hogs were also the source of much of the meat they consumed. Some of it was preserved by canning; the sausage, ham and bacon preserved by smoking. And of course there were chickens. They kept three milk cows to supply their own milk, cream, and butter. There is no mention of producing milk for sale. Any skimming was done by hand, the skim milk fed to the hogs, and the cream used as such or made into butter. Initially, Benjamin purchased feeder cattle and fattened them for the Chicago market. But as the region became increasingly dairy-oriented, feeder cattle became less available and he turned to raising sheep for wool and meat to sell. Also, he usually had a three or four year old gelding being raised for sale. They commanded a good price from urban dwellers that used them for their coaches.

They had a number of horses, and they supplied the power for plowing, transportation, and heavy lifting. Plowing was done with a single-bottom 14" walking plow pulled by a team of two horses. The family had a carriage, a buggy, and at least one wagon—all horse-drawn.

Benjamin's father, Nathaniel, "raised a lot of pigs and he had most of the farm fenced 'hog tight.' There were many rail fences—split-oak rails about twelve feet long and uneven in shape, roughly triangular, say four or five inches on a side, and laid zig-zag." These were replaced with wire fences over a period of time.

Stephen Switzer believed that Benjamin built the large corncrib and the scale house. A 1941 photo shows only the house, barn, crib, scale house and windmill tower over the well (though small out buildings may be obscured by trees). Also, approximately 500 feet SW of the house is a gravel "pit" in the hillside. Another source of cash? And begun by whom?

Benjamin decided to move to Nebraska where his wife had relatives and he purchased land there in 1910. The sale of the Illinois farm and the move were accomplished in December of 1911.

Chart I: Descendants of Nathaniel Jennings Barmore

Nathaniel Jennings Barmore
  b. 2.11.1828 Greene Co. PA
  d. 12.15.1911 Stephenson Co. IL
m. 12.9.1851 Twin Grove WI
  Susanna Stair
  b. 11.18.1831 Tippecanoe Co. IN
  d. 11.14.1921 Whittier CA

Salome Elizabeth Barmore
    9.5.1852 WI–11.15.1945 IL
m. 12.10.1874 Stephenson Co. IL
    Thomas Henry Cahoon
    7.3.1849 PA–11.1.1897 IL
	William Harrison Cahoon
	Mary Alice Cahoon
	Susan Maria Cahoon
	Jennings Gilbert Cahoon
	Geneva Jeanette Cahoon
	Elsie Mae Cahoon
	Ruth Irene Cahoon

Frank Gapen Barmore
    11.25.1854 IL–3.9.1939 IL
m. 2.5.1879 near Freeport IL
    Sarah Ella Yarger
    12.11.1852 PA–1.18.1939
	Beulah Allison Barmore
	Myrtle Ellen Barmore
	Zella Ruth Barmore
	Roy Ethol Barmore
	Floyd Glenn Barmore
	Clarence Verl Barmore

Mary Kezia Barmore
    1.16.1857 IL–3.3.1930 CA
m. 2.14.1878 Stephenson Co. IL
    Benjamin Franklin Chambers
    2.14.1855 IL–3.13.1930 CA
	Robert Lloyd Chambers
	Edwin Barmore Chambers
	Jennings Glenn Chambers
	Mary Elizabeth Chambers

William Barmore 3.29.1859 IL–2.21.1861 IL	

Jacob Stair Barmore
12.9.1861 IL–10.14.1933 CA
m. 1.26.1893 Freeport IL
Jennie Belle Reitzell
1.26.1870 IL–5.26.1937 CA

Paul Reitzell Barmore
Margaret Isabelle Barmore
Esther Lucile Barmore
Karl Jennings Barmore
Jacob Leonard Barmore

Willard Patchin Barmore
5.8.1864 IL–4.27.1871 IL

Jennie Jennings Barmore
11.21.1867 IL–5.12.1964 CA
m. 12.29.1892 Stephenson Co. IL
Harrison Lincoln Raymer
12.13.1865 IL–4.15.1958 CA

Benjamin Bradshaw Barmore
6.10.1870 IL–7.10.1954 CA
m(1) 12.21.1893 Freeport IL
Addie Louella Gorr
4.12.1873 IL–6.20.1938 CA
m(2) 7.16.1939 Whittier CA
Mayme (Yargar) Fleming
12.3.1875 IL–7.21.1954 CA

John Jennings Barmore
Lawrence Arthur Barmore
Merrill Gorr Barmore
Leanna Barmore
Mark Alfred Barmore*
Lorene Alice Barmore

Ruth Anna Barmore
2.25.1873 IL–5.23.1969 IA
m. 1.31.1895 Stephenson Co. IL
John Franklin Gift
10.31.1869 IL–5.9.1951 IA

Lois Marguerite Gift
Hazel Evelyn Gift
William Lester Gift
Harry Barmore Gift
Ethel Faye Gift
Dorothy Pauline Gift
Gladys Lorene Gift
Robert Eldon Gift

*Father of Frank E. Barmore

Table I: Land Transactions

Transactions involving Nathaniel Jennings Barmore and his descendants and lands in either Rock Grove Township or Oneco Township, Stephenson Co., Illinois. The dates are the dates of the transactions, not the recording dates.

No.	Date	Buyers and Sellers Land description and comments	Acreage	Price
1	1858.02.25	N. Jennings Barmore from Jessie & Elizabeth Starr; SW-¼ and NE-¼ of NW-¼, S27, T29N, R8E.	80 acres	$700
2	1858.12.05	N. Jennings Barmore from Daniel & Hannah Starr SE-¼ of NW-¼, S27, T29N, R8E.	40 acres	$250
3	1867.12.16	N. Jennings Barmore from John F. Reynolds; NW-¼ of NW-¼, S27, T29N, R8E.	40 acres	$1,200
4	1871.03.31	N. Jennings Barmore from Noah & Mary Smith; a complexly shaped plot in S22, T29N, R8E, (see next transaction)	135.1 acres	$3,850
5	1872.04.04	N. Jennings & Susan Barmore to John H. C. Kline all of (4) except a 41 acre plot, 106 rod N-S x 61.9 rod E-W, in the SW portion of the E-½ of SW-¼, S22, T29N, R8E.	94.1 acres	$2,800
6	1874.11.25	N. Jennings Barmore from Thomas & Jane McCanley; NW-¼ of SW-¼ and W-½ of SW-¼ of SW-¼, all in S27, T29N, R8E.	60 acres	$3600
7	1884.April	N. Jennings & Susan Barmore to Church Trustees i.e. Trustees of the Pleasant Hill Methodist-Episcopal Church, a plot of land in the SW corner of NW-¼, S27, T29N, R8E, 8.54 rods N-S x 6.32 rods E-W, adjacent to and East of a similar sized plot that held the Pleasant Hill School which straddled the Oneco-Rock Grove town line.	⅓ acre	25¢
8	1886.spring	N. Jennings & Susan Barmore to Thomas H. Cahoon; NW-¼ of SW-¼ and W-½ of SW-¼ of SW-¼, both in S27, T29N, R8E.	60 acres	$4,100
9	1886.11.15	Thomas H. Cahoon from David & Elisie E. Zimmerman E-½ of SW-¼ of SW-¼, S27, T29N, R8E.	20 acres	$1,200

10a	1892.09.26	Jacob Stair Barmore from heirs of Ira Winchell; SE-¼ of NE-¼, S32 and SW-¼ of NW-¼, S33, both in T29N, R8E.	80 acres	$2800
10b	1892.09.26	N. Jennings Barmore from heirs of Ira Winchell; W-½ of NE-¼ and NE-¼ of NE-¼, both in S32, T29N, R8E	120 acres	$6,000
10c	1892.09.26	Benjamin Bradshaw Barmore from heirs of Ira Winchell NW-¼ of NW-¼, S33, T29N, R8E.	40 acres	$1,200
11	1892.11.30	N. Jennings & Susan Barmore to Frank G. Barmore E-½ of NW-¼, S27, T29N, R8E.	80 acres	$5,400
12	1893.11.02	Benjamin Bradshaw Barmore to Jacob Stair Barmore NW-¼ of NW-¼, S33, T29N, R8E.	40 acres	$1,350
13a	1897.05.03	Thomas H. & Salome E. Cahoon to N. Jennings Barmore SW-¼ of SW-¼, S27, T29N, R8E.	40 acres	$2,400
13b	1897.09.28	Thomas H. & Salome E. Cahoon to N. Jennings Barmore NW-¼ of SW-¼, S27, T29N, R8E.	40 acres	$3,000
14	1899.03.16	Frank G. Barmore from David Zimmerman's widow & heirs NE-¼ of SW-¼, S27, T29N, R8E.	40 acres	$2,560
15a	1903.03.23	N. Jennings & Susan Barmore to Salome E. Cahoon SW-¼ of SW-¼, S27, T29N, R8E.	40 acres	$2,400
15b	1903.03.25	N. Jennings & Susan Barmore to Jacob S. Barmore NE-¼ of NE-¼, S32, T29N, R8E.	40 acres	$3,000
15c	1903.03.25	N. Jennings & Susan Barmore to Benjamin B. Barmore W-½ of NW-¼, S27 and a 41 acre plot, 106 rod N-S x 61.9 rod E-W, located in the SW portion of the E-½ of SW-¼, S22, T29N, R8E.	121 acres	$7,865
16	1907.10.09	Jacob S. & Jennie B. Barmore to John W. Bridge; W-½ of NW-¼, S33 and E-½ of NE-¼, S32, both in T29N, R8E.	160 acres	$14,600
17	1909.03.27	Jacob S. Barmore from Marie F. & Ralph W. Moore NW-¼, S31, T29N, R8E, except a 7 acre parcel in the NW corner.	153 acres	$20,000

18	1911.12.18	Benjamin B. & Addie L. Barmore to Elmer & Anna Denny; W-½ of NW-¼, S27 and a 41 acre plot, 106 rod N-S x 61.9 rod E-W, located in the SW portion of the E-½ of SW-¼, S22, both in T29N, R8E. (In 1916 this land was acquired by Charles H. Allison and later was transferred to Allison's son-in-law and daughter, Stephen & Elva Switzer.)	121 acres	$13,733
19	1912.02.16	N. Jennings Barmore's widow & heirs to Salome E. Cahoon; NW-¼ of SW-¼, in S27, T29N, R8E by Quit Claims Deed.	40 acres	$1
20	1914.02.10	N. Jennings Barmore's heirs to John A. & Clay B. Bridges W-½ of NE-¼, S32, T29N, R8E.	80 acres	$8,000

Notes

Adam Starr and Levi Starr (presumed to be the son of Adam Starr) came to Clarno Township, Green County, Wisconsin, around 1835-1836 (see Bingham, p. 141). Adam purchased approximately 400 acres of public land in the township in 1839 (see Government Land Office records), some of which was adjacent to land acquired by Jacob Stair, father of Nathaniel's wife, Susan. Levi purchased 400 acres of public land nearby in Wisconsin and Illinois in 1839, 1845, 1847, and 1849. Daniel Starr and Elizabeth Starr, wife of Jessie Starr, purchased 40 acres each of public land in Illinois in 1845 and 1847 respectively (Jessie and Daniel are presumed to be sons of Adam Starr). Forty of the 80 acres purchased by Nathaniel from Jessie Starr and the 40 acres purchased from John F. Reynolds were originally part of Levi's Illinois public land purchases. In the 1855 Wisconsin State Census, Joseph Barmore is listed next to Levi Starr. Clearly the Starr family was well known to the Barmore family.

Though Stair is sometimes misspelled as Starr in various records, these are two unrelated families. The Stair family came to the area from Virginia via Indiana while the Starr family came to the area from North Carolina via Ohio (see Federal Census returns, Population Schedules).

Table II: Productions of Agriculture Schedules, 1860, 1870, 1880 Census returns for Nathaniel Jennings Barmore, Rock Grove Township., Stephenson Co., Illinois.

Entries: N.J.B. = N.B. = Nathaniel Jennings Barmore; F.G.B. = Frank Gapen Barmore; T.H.C. = Thomas Henry Cahoon, husband of Salome Elizabeth Barmore. xx = not asked in that Census; - = no entry. The list of questions asked in the different Censuses varies as does their order.

Column Heading	units	1860	1870	1880	1880
Name of "Farmer(s)" (see note below)	-	N.J.B.	N.J.B.	N.B.	F.G.B T.H.C
Land, improved (all)	acres	120	160	xx	xx
Land, improved, tilled	acres	xx	xx	260	90
Land, improved, perm. meadow, etc.	acres	xx	xx	20	-
Land, unimproved (all)	acres	20	xx	xx	xx
Land, unimproved, woodland	acres	xx	20	20	-
Land, unimproved, other	acres	xx	-	-	-
Cash value of Farm	$$	5,000	9,000	14,000	-
Value of implements & Machinery	$$	150	280	200	300
Value of wages pd. incld. board	$$	xx	192	20	-
Weeks hired labor (excld. house work)	num.	xx	xx	-	-
Cost of fences built or repaired	$$	xx	xx	-	-
Cost of fertilizers in 1879	$$	xx	xx	-	-
Horses	num.	5	5	6	5
Asses & Mules	num.	-	-	-	-
Milch cows	num.	1	7	3	7
Working oxen	num.	-	-	-	-
Other cattle	num.	10	8	13	5
Cattle, calves dropped	num.	xx	xx	3	4
Cattle, purchased	num.	xx	xx	-	1
Cattle, sold living	num.	xx	xx	1	1
Cattle, slaughtered	num.	xx	xx	-	-
Cattle, lost - all causes	num.			-	-
Sheep	num.	-	7	-	-
Sheep (all other questions for 1880)	-	xx	xx	-	-
Swine	num.	6	22	55	35
Value of livestock	$$	630	865	900	600
Poultry, on hand (excld. spring hatching)	num.	xx	xx	50	100
Poultry, other	num.	xx	xx	-	130
Eggs produced in 1879	Doz.	xx	xx	50	100

Column Heading (*cont.*)	units	1860	1870	1880	1880
Wheat, Area	acres	xx	xx	-	-
Wheat, (all)	bushels	600	xx	-	-
Wheat, Spring	bushels	xx	390	xx	xx
Wheat, Winter	bushels	xx	-	xx	xx
Rye, Area	acres	xx	xx	10	10
Rye	bushels	-	75	110	110
Indian Corn, Area	acres	xx	xx	35	70
Indian Corn	bushels	800	1,200	1,100	2,200
Oats, Area	acres	xx	xx	20	40
Oats	bushels	500	400	600	1,400
Rice	lbs.	-	-	xx	xx
Tobacco	lbs.	-	-	-	-
Ginned Cotton	Bales	-	-	xx	xx
Wool (all questions)	lbs.	-	21	-	-
Peas & Beans	bushels	-	-	-	-
Irish Potatoes, Area (see note)	acres	xx	xx	-	1.5
Irish Potatoes	bushels	15	40	10	95
Sweet Potatoes (all questions)	bushels	-	-	-	-
Barley (all questions)	bushels	-	-	-	-
Buckwheat (all questions)	bushels	-	-	-	-
Apple Orchard, Area	acres	xx	xx	2	-
Apple Orchard, Bearing Trees	num.	xx	xx	50	-
Peach Orchard (all questions)	various	xx	xx	-	-
Value of orchard products (see note)	$$	-	15	-	-
Nurseries (all questions)	various	xx	xx	-	-
Wine & Vineyard (all questions)	various	-	-	-	-
Value of Market Garden produce	$$	-	-	-	-
Butter	lbs.	300	525	100	150
Cheese	lbs.	-	-	-	-
Milk sold	gallons	-	-	-	-
Grass Land, Mown	acres	xx	xx	10	-
Grass Land, Not Mown	acres	xx	xx	-	-
Hay	tons	7	16	15	-
Clover Seed	bushels	-	-	19	-
Grass Seed	bushels	-	-	-	-
Hops (all questions)	various	-	-	-	-
Hemp (all questions)	tons	-	-	-	-
Flax (all questions)	lbs.	-	-	-	-

Column Heading (*cont.*)	units	1860	1870	1880	1880
Broom Corn (all questions)	various	xx	xx	-	-
Silk Cocoons	lbs.	-	-	xx	xx
Maple Sugar	lbs.	-	-	-	-
Cane Sugar	Hhds. of 1,000 lbs.	-	-	-	-
Molasses	gallons	-	10	-	-
Beeswax	lbs.	-	-	-	-
Honey	lbs.	-	-	25	-
Forest Products, wood cut	cords	xx	xx	10	10
Forest Products	$$	xx	-	20	20
Value of home made manufacture	$$	-	-	xx	xx
Value of animals slaughtered	$$	270	608	xx	xx
Value of all production, betterments and additions to livestock	$$	xx	1,920	xx	xx
Value of all farm production in 1879 (sold, consumed or on hand)	$$	xx	xx	1,800	800

Notes

a) In the 1880 census N. J. Barmore is given as the owner of 260 acres, while F. G. Barmore and T. H. Cahoon (a son and son-in-law of N. J. Barmore) are renting land (for shares of the products rather than cash). Land records and the sequence of entries in the census schedule imply that the land rented is adjacent to and owned by N.J.B. Some of the entries are more comprehensible when considering the entries for all three "farmers," hence the double column for 1880, where the last column combines the entries for F.G.B. and T.H.C.

b) In the 1880 census, N.J.B. paid $20 for farm labor during 1879 but there is no entry for the number of weeks labor was hired.

c) In the 1880 census N.J.B., apparently for receiving only a 20% share of the produce, used a half acre owned by a neighbor, Meyers Addison. Thus, N.J.B., in spite of having no acreage in potatoes, "produced" 10 bushels of potatoes during 1879, Addison produced the remaining 40 bushels.

d) In the 1880 census, N.J.B. had 50 bearing apple trees in a 2 acre orchard, yet had no orchard produce of value for 1879. One wonders why.

III. The House

The house and barn were so typical of farmhouses and barns of their time and place and of how they changed that it seemed worthwhile to record something of their character. In 1977 and 1979 some photographs, measurements, and sketches of them and their features were made. In addition there were visits in 1964 and 1970 and several other photographs. The drawings are based on these sources of information, but are not "measured drawings" in the usual sense. Notation in parentheses refers to the elevations, plans, details, and section views of the two buildings or their parts. The drawings are at various scales—all the plans (except P1) at a small scale, all the elevations (E and P1) at an intermediate scale, most of the details (D) at a large scale, and sections (S and a few detail drawings, D) at a much larger scale. When dimensions are given they are measured, not nominal, unless otherwise qualified. Some comments follow.

The house is located near the middle of the northern edge of the SW-¼ of the NW-¼ of Sec. 27. It can be seen on large-scale USGS topographic maps, in air-photos and satellite images at Long. 89°34'19" West and Lat. 42°29'09" North. The house is placed on ground gently rising to the north. The "front" of the house faces south and faces the lane to the farm from the east-west public road approximately ⅕ mile distant. The house is centered on the axis of the lane.

The house has evolved over the years and the original appearance and plan are not known with certainty. Jennings Cahoon told Stephen Switzer that his father, Thomas Cahoon (d. 1897), remembered that originally the west part of the house was only one story high. There is evidence of this in the attic framing in the west portion, which is quite different from that in the east portion. Also, the wainscoting in the alcove containing "Grandma's bay window" (d, P1) differs from that in the rest of the room and Stephen Switzer comments that the alcove's west wall was of different construction. Lastly, the window in the alcove differs in proportion, trim, and construction from others in the house.

Several things suggest that the entrance (D13, P1) into the largest, most elaborate room is the "main" front entrance. The knob/latch box/lock on the door is substantial, with a white opal glass or white china knob and black box (D14). A paved walk (later, not visible in a 1901 photograph), a yard fence gate and the lane to the farm all line up with the door that, in turn, is in the center of the front facade.

There is an additional front entrance (D1, P1, E2, E3) in the southeast room. The trim of this door is much more elaborate than trim elsewhere—resplendent in its classical motifs. There are pilasters on either side to form columns, complete with bases (S1), fluted shafts (S4), and capitals (S2) with the whole surmounted with an entablature (S3) composed of architrave, frieze, and cornice. The doorstop is richly detailed (S5 and portions of S4). This embellishment suggests that this door is a formal front entrance, opening into what was perhaps a formal parlor.

This formal entrance is sheltered by a very decorative small porch (ca. 66" wide x 72" deep) with bench seats on either side. However, this porch obscures and crowds the door and the windows on either side of it. The ends of the cornice above the door and above the adjacent windows are clipped off by the porch. The entablature supporting the porch roof is similar, if not identical to that above the door. The classical portions of this porch argue for it being part of the original construction while the crowding, bench seats, and the (surely later) Victorian decorative posts, etc. argue for it being either modified or added later.

Hence the original appearance of the house as built in 1867 may have been somewhat as shown in E1. I believe that the formal entrance (D1) in the east (right) wing is coeval with the house, but I cannot prove it—hence the question mark. Was the southwestern room originally its current size or was it expanded to enclose a portion of the porch when the alcove (d, P1) was added to the main room? Examples of both constructions are common in the studies mentioned below. Either way, in the west (left) wing there must have been one or two windows in the south wall, but there is no proof. Hence the other question mark on E1. The appearance of the porch roof is conjectural. It could have been a separate roof or a continuation of the main roof as shown. There must have been chimneys or stove pipes (c, E1). The windows and the main door are assumed to be the same as they are shown many years later in a 1901 photograph. The shutters may also have been there since the beginning.

Such facades seem ubiquitous in the upper Midwest—examples appear in nostalgic watercolors of weathered farmhouses, photographic collections (see the University of Wisconsin-La

Crosse Murphy Library Special Collections), and scholarly studies. Talbot Hamlin (see Hamlin) displays a facade and floor plan of an 1850 farmhouse recorded by the Historic American Buildings Survey that is eerily similar in appearance, floor plan, and dimensions. Another scholar would call it a T-Plan or Type 4 farmhouse in his typology (see Peterson). A third would call it an Upright-and-Wing or Lazy-T farmhouse in his classification (see Noble).

On December 9, 1901, Nathaniel and Susanna celebrated their fiftieth wedding anniversary. A photograph of more than sixty attending family members and friends in front of the house reveals the appearance of the house at that time. Its original Greek Revival style has been modified with the addition of some Victorian gingerbread trim (D7, E2, E3). The portion of the original house visible in the photograph is shown in E2.

A small, one-story addition (j, P2) had been built around 1894 and remained on the house until about 1903, as mentioned above. The approximate sizes of the components of this temporary addition are based on the 1901 photograph and a sketch by John Jennings Barmore made a half-century later. The photograph shows the appearance. The south facade contained a door and one window and is similar in appearance to the rest of the building at the time but the trim about the door and window is simpler. And there is no gingerbread decoration. No trace remains of this addition.

A one-story wing, around 16' x 28' or 30' extended to the north from the west end of the north wall (k: P1, P2, P4). Stephen Switzer said that the quality of its construction and its condition was much worse than the rest of the house. This suggests that this wing was not part of the original house. The date this was added to the house is unknown. John Jennings Barmore recalled that while he lived there (1895–1911) it contained a kitchen, summer kitchen, and wood shed. In 1970 it was demolished and replaced with a modern addition.

In the twentieth century there were more changes. In the first floor windows a single pane of glass replaced the 2 x 3 lights in each sash. Manufactured composite siding replaced or covered the older clapboards and some of the classical trim. The appearance of the house in the late 1970s is shown in E3. Some comments follow.

In the basement there is no cellar floor save earth. The walls are flat stones laid in mortar. The wall rises to the level of the first floor, hence enclosing the beam ends and floor joist ends, and hiding the sills in all but a few cracks. In the east end of the south wall even the cross bracing between joists is enclosed in the masonry. In the east wall there is a 4' wide, walled-up entrance beginning about 18" off the floor (e, P2). A board wall divides the space. These two features are probably from the time when the building was shared by the two families. The interior stairs into the basement consist of ten steps of 9" rise and 8" run. There are also exterior stairs to the cellar at the west end of the house.

The framing of the original portion of the house is positively medieval with post-and-beam and mortise-and-tenon construction. In the attic of the east wing a little of the original framing can be seen. The slope of the roof is 7/12, rise over run (which equals approximately 30°). There is no ridgepole or ridge board. The sheeting on the roof is made up of ¾" oak boards, random widths, some 19" to 22" wide. The rafters are 2" x 6" on 24" centers. The top plate is squared up with an ax or adz, of oak and 6" x 6". At the corners, the top plates are connected with a lap joint, probably pegged (not accessible to view). The ceiling joists have tenons and the top plate is notched and mortised to receive them (D5). The studs, at least some of oak, are 2" x 3¾" on 16" centers. The exterior wall sheeting boards run vertically.

The main beams for the first floor are of white oak, also squared up with an ax or adz. The sills are the same. The main beams are 9¼" wide x 7¾" deep and are mortised to receive the joist's tenons (D6, P3). The joists are ca. 2¼" x 7¾" on 24" centers and display the straight, regular vertical saw marks of milled lumber cut by a reciprocating saw (in contrast to a band saw or circular saw).

In the attic of the west wing (the second floor of which was added later), more modern or balloon framing is visible. Roof sheeting is ¾" x 8". Other components are 1¾" x 3¾" or 1⅝" x 3⅝" on 16" or 24" centers. Everything appears very regular and composed of milled, modern, dimensioned lumber.

The exterior measures 24' 3½" x 40'4¾". But note, either the house has spread or the floor joists have shrunk by about 4"—the tenons on the floor joists have pulled out of their mortices in the main beams by an amount that totals about 4". (The joists are now supported on angle iron bolted to the beams.) Modern siding plus expansion is enough to account for the size of the house in excess of 24' x 40' which I believe to be its original intended dimension. The west wing is 24' x 24' and the east wing is 16' x 24'.

The 1901 photograph shows: clapboards (approximately 5¼" exposed); shutters (a, E2; now gone); Greek revival trim (b, E2), especially the "formal" entrance (D1) and the window architrave and cornice (D8); and Victorian gingerbread (D7). The gingerbread seems a little out of place. It is not likely to be coeval with the rest of the house. The main exterior door trim is the same as the typical exterior window trim, both displaying classical profiles. The clapboards are gone or covered and the siding is now a modern composition siding with approximately 10 ⅝" exposed. All the windows were of 2 x 3 lights in each sash (D10). Those on the ground floor later had a single pane in each sash (D8, D9). The second floor windows are ca. 7" shorter vertically. The attic window and vent (D3, D4) appear alternately in the north and south walls at different dates.

In the interior, the main and largest room is more elaborately finished than the others with wainscoting and some plain molding at the height of the door top trim (D12, D13). There is a blocked hole in the ceiling near e' (P1). Stephen Switzer has noted very heavy floor wear near there and supposed this was because a kitchen stove was located there and the room originally was used as the kitchen. Since around 1900 a year-round kitchen was in the northwestern wing of the house. In the western section of the house there is an abandoned stairway to the second floor (above the interior cellar stairs). It is boarded over at the second floor level. This probably dates from the period when two families shared the house (from around 1893–1903). The subfloor is ⅞" x 5¼" tongue-and-groove lumber, showing circular saw marks. There is no finished floor save for linoleum or vinyl floor covering in some rooms. The earlier brick chimneys were mounted on wall brackets ca. 60" above the second floor (g, P4) and fed by stove pipes from the rooms below (e, e', P1, P4). As the second floor in the west wing is not original, one can only wonder if the chimneys through the roof were stovepipe or similarly supported brick. The brick chimneys were taken down above the roof line between 1964 and 1976 (c', E3). A modern chimney to serve a furnace in the basement was located outside on the north wall.

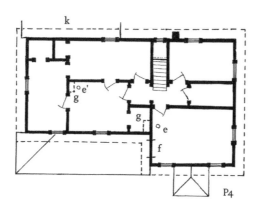

P4

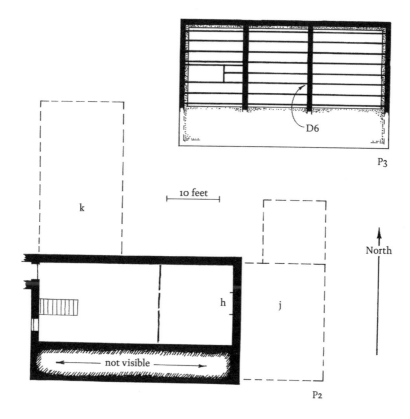

D6

P3

10 feet

k

North

h   j

not visible

P2

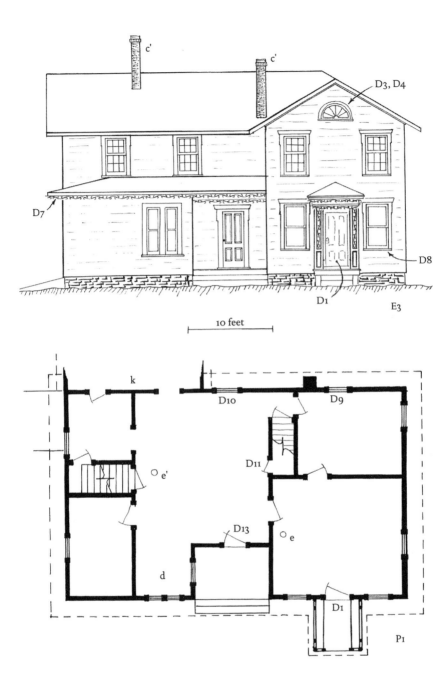

c' c'

D3, D4

D7

D8

D1

E3

10 feet

k

D10 D9

D11

e'

D13

e

d

D1

P1

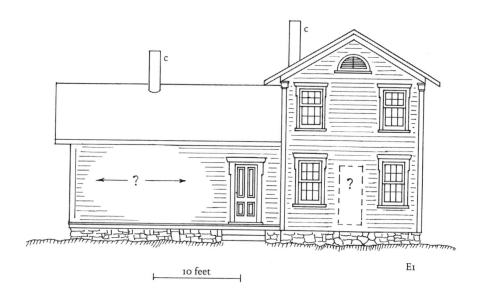

10 feet

E1

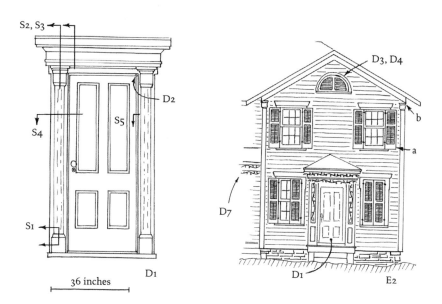

S2, S3

D2

S4

S5

S1

36 inches

D1

D3, D4

b

a

D7

D1

E2

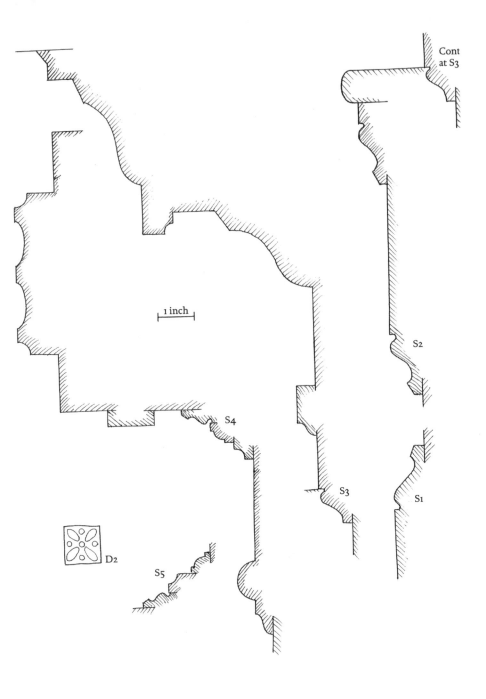

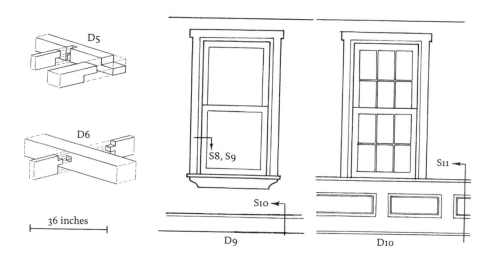

36 inches

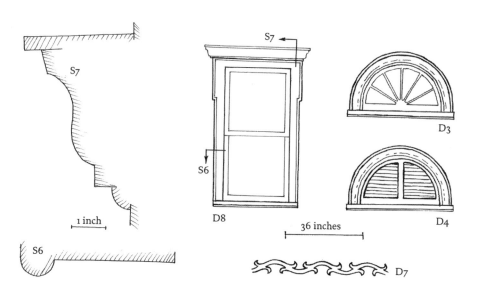

1 inch

36 inches

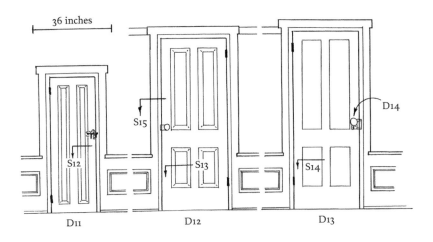

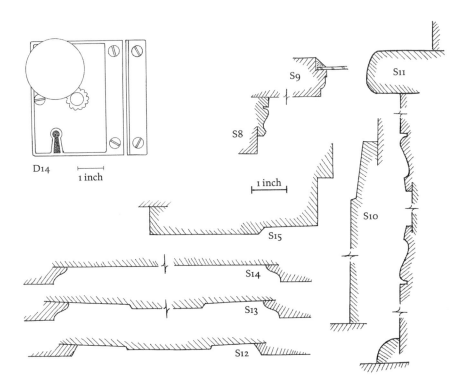

IV. The Barn

The barn on the farm is believed to have been completed in the same year as the house, in 1867. This barn is an excellent example of its kind and is often called a Pennsylvania Bank Barn. While the basement of the barn has been modified, enough traces are left to indicate its original form. The upper level preserves its original form and has one feature that is uncommon if not unique. Using the very well developed Ensminger classification, the barn is a Closed-Forebay Standard [Pennsylvania Bank] Barn, Class II, Type A (Dornbusch Type H) (see Ensminger, page 56 and Appendix B). Ensminger's work is, if not the last word on Pennsylvania Barns, at least a leading authoritative statement on the subject. His terminology (see his glossary) will be used in the comments that follow.

The barn, like the house, faces south on ground rising to the north. The higher ground on the north side (the bank) allows for a gentle earthen ramp (z; P5, P6, P7) leading to large rolling double doors into the upper level of the barn. The west, north, and east basement walls of the barn are randomly laid fieldstone. The original south basement wall (stable front wall) has been moved outward to be flush with the front wall of the barn's upper level. However, there is clear evidence (given below) of its location, which was recessed five feet under the cantilevered front wall of the barn's upper level, the forebay. The basement's east and west stone walls extend beyond the original south wall to the location of the front wall of the barn's upper level, thus forming the closed-forebay. There were originally at least two windows in each of the east and west basement walls.

Externally the basement measures about 42' 5" east-west by 35' 2" north-south. The roof ridge runs east-west and is centered from north to south. The roof slopes are equal at about 30°. The east and west walls are thus the gable walls which are symmetrical about their centers. The symmetrical profile and the cantilevered forebay are some of the hallmarks of the standard Pennsylvania barn.

All four walls of the upper level are wood. The siding is composed of boards placed vertically. The walls are pierced by over two dozen rectangular wooden-louvered ventilation openings. In the 1970s the siding was "barn red" and the trim for the ventilation openings was white. The only other decorative elements on the exterior are a pair of openings high in the gable walls near the peak each of which combines a small window with a more elaborate ventilation opening in a form that echoes the classical revival Palladian window (D25).

Stephenson County is unusually rich in barns of this type (see Price and Sculle). The interior framing and structure of this barn display much that is significant. While most of this is revealed in the drawings that follow, several comments about them are needed.

Most of the drawings represent the original 1867 character of the barn. The exceptions are the plan, P7 and elevation, E5, which represent twentieth-century appearances. The drawings of the barn, like those for the house, are drawn at various scales. The drawings concentrate on the framing and they do not show everything. For example, the ventilation openings are indicated in the plan view of the upper level (P6) and in the elevation views of the bents and walls (E4, E8, E9) but not when they would otherwise appear in section views. Likewise, the siding is shown only when seen face on, but not when seen edge on. In contrast, the doors are only shown edge on in the plan views. For the rolling doors, the dotted line indicates the track above them from which they are hung. The shingles are not shown at all and the roof shingle nailing strips are only hinted at in one drawing (r, E4). The upper-level floorboards are not shown at all. Some of the framing joints are shown in the detail drawings D15–D24, some are section views or top view projections, others are isometric drawings. Many of the joints are pegged with wood pins indicated by dots. Not all joints and pegging are illustrated. Some joints and pegging were not accessible to view. Some joints were so closely fitted they could not be probed.

At some point the basement was converted to facilitate milking of a dairy herd. There is no indication that either Nathaniel or Benjamin Barmore had more than a few milk cows or produced milk for sale or cheese making. This arrangement in dairy barns was not often used until the second or third decade of the twentieth century (see Ensminger, p. 257, citing others). Benjamin sold the farm in 1911, and I conclude that this conversion was later than 1911.

The original basement plan is shown in P5. There may have been a third window in the east and west walls (q, P5, E4). There would be a need for light in the original basement, there is adequate space for them, and three windows would match the three louvered ventilation openings above in the upper-level gable walls. However, that portion of each wall was removed when the basement was remodeled and any evidence that might have existed has been lost. In the conversion large doors were cut into the east and west basement walls and one window in each wall filled in (p, P7, E4). The 11" x 11" posts that supported the summer beams were replaced with approximately 5" diameter steel posts. The size of the original posts is indicated by the impression they left on the summer beams and the size of the mortices in those beams. The southern summer beam (n, E4, E5) was shifted toward the south. The original arrangement of the stalls and other features in the basement and the structure and appearance of the stable front wall (south basement wall) are unknown—hence the large question mark on the plan, P5.

The southernmost beam that supported the cantilevered forebay was removed and a new beam installed supported by a substantial set of posts that formed the new front (south) wall, flush with the south wall of the forebay above (m, E4, E5). The size and position of the original beam is indicated by the still visible impressions it made on the forebay beams above. And the position is also indicated by the finishing of the forebay beams. Those beams run the full depth of the barn and inside the original barn they are finished to the proper thickness by flattening the top and bottom while the sides were left untouched and semi-round with the bark left on. But the exposed ends supporting the cantilevered forebay are squared up on all four sides and even finished off by chamfering the edges along what would have been the exposed five-foot length. The north ends of these beams are joined to the sill in the north wall with a mortise-and-tenon joint (D18) that resembles the joint (D5) in the house. The sill supporting the south wall of the upper level rests on top of the forebay beams and sills on the east and west basement walls.

At some point an opening was made in the basement wall to access a later (and now nonexistent) silo (x, P7) near the northwest corner of the barn. Access to the recent milk house (y, P7) near the northeast corner was created by expanding one of the original basement window openings to become a doorway. The plan of the basement in the late 1970s is shown in P7.

The upper level of the barn consists of four bents dividing the space into three bays (P6, E4, E6–E9). All elevations are views inside the barn. The elevations E4–E7 are views looking west. The elevation E8 is a view looking south. The elevation E9 is a view looking north. The roof rafters on each side are composed of two lengths, meeting at the purlin (D15). The rafter spacing varies between 25" and 26". Like the house, there is no ridge pole or ridge board. The bents are so-called H-bents, not to be confused with either the H-frames or the Dornbusch Type H barns (see Ensminger, p. 264). The western bay is the mow, separated from the thrashing bay by the mowstead bent. The mowstead bent supports a mowstead rail (s, E6, the northern third now missing) and wall (t, E6) composed of horizontal planks nailed on. There are now two hay holes (u, P6) in the mow floor. The southern one may be original, the northern one surely is. The eastern bay is half the width of the other two and is divided up into grain bins. The bins are formed by loose planks (w, E7–E9) dropped into slots (D21, D22), allowing their height to be adjusted as the bins are filled or emptied. The location of these grain bins is unusual for a standard Pennsylvania barn. They are usually located in the forebay (see Ensminger, p. 67). The bent between the grain bins and the thrashing bay contains three short beams (v, E7) which now support joists which in turn support a floor, creating a mezzanine haymow above the grain bins. The east wall bent was hidden by hay and grain and for the most part not observed. As it must help support the mezzanine mow and the planks forming the grain bins, I would expect that it is much like the bent shown in E7, with the upper portions looking like the upper part of the west wall bent (E4).

All the large frame members in the original barn are oak and finished off with an ax or adz. Frame members 4" x 4" or smaller and the boards and planks appear to be milled lumber. All the large beams are continuous except for the southern purlin, which is spliced with a scarf joint (D24) over a purlin post (queen post). The large frame members are ca. 8½" square. The purlins and queen posts are 7½" square. Three short beams (v, E7) are ca. 6" x 8". The forebay beams are about 8½" thick but various widths. The sills on the top of the basement walls are about 8½" thick but noticeably wider. The summer beams supporting the forebay beams are 11" x 11" as were their supporting posts.

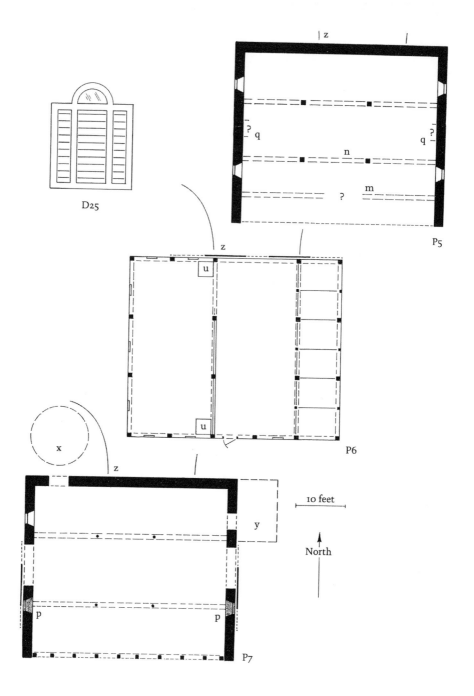

D25

z

q ?

? q

n

? m

P5

z

u

u

P6

x

z

y

10 feet

North

p

p

P7

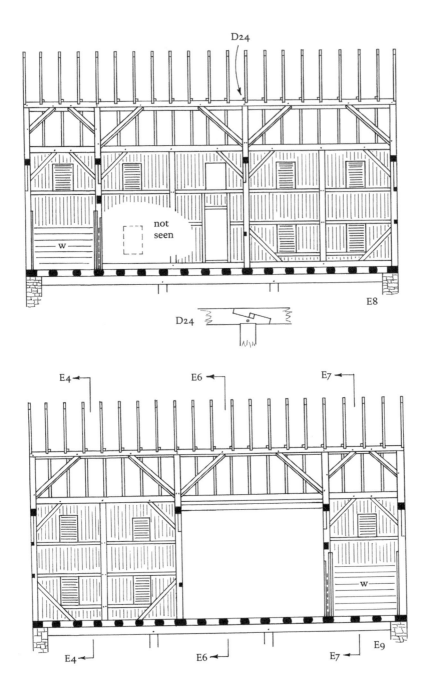

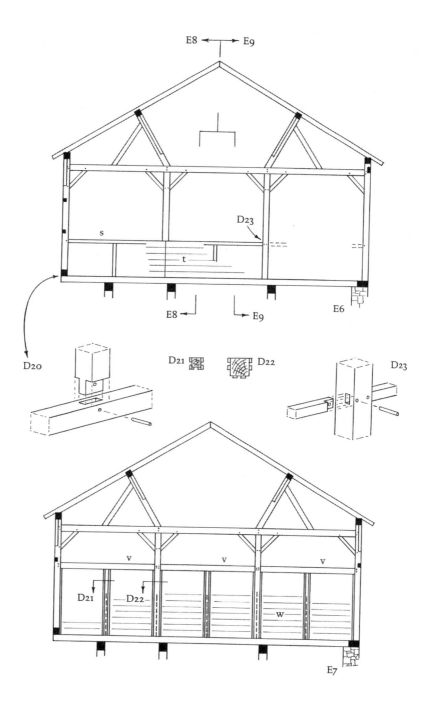

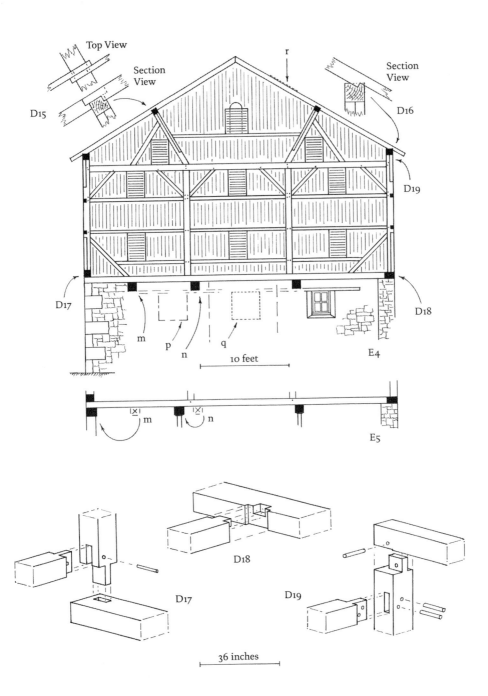

Top View

Section
View

D15

Section
View

D16

r

D19

D17

m

p

n

q

10 feet

E4

D18

m

n

E5

D18

D17

D19

36 inches

References

Frank E. Barmore, *The Descendants of Joseph Barmore, 1792–1874*. Unpublished manuscript. A penultimate version of the final draft was microfilmed 1970. The microfilm copy is available at the State Historical Society of Wisconsin (Madison), Microfilm P82–3333.

Ruth A. Barmore, *The Descendants of Nathaniel Jennings Barmore & Susanna Stair: Statistical Data* (Whittier, Calif.: Ruth A. Barmore, 1964). Copies available: a) Freeport (Illinois) Public Library, Hist 929.2 Barmore; b) State Historical Society of Wisconsin (Madison), Pamphlet Collection 68–1897.

Helen M. Bingham, *History of Green County, Wisconsin* (Milwaukee, Wisc.: Burdick & Armitage printers, 1877).

C. T. Dunham, *Map of the County of Stephenson, Illinois* (New York: C. T. Dunham, 1859). Ca. 53 x 60 inches. 1:39,600 = 50 chains/inch = 200 rods/inch. Note: Surveyed and drawn by C. T. Dunham, under the direction of H. F. Walling. Engraved, printed, colored & mounted at H. F. Walling's Map Establishment.

Robert F. Ensminger, *The Pennsylvania Barn: Its Origin, Evolution, and Distribution in North America*, 2nd ed. (Baltimore: John Hopkins University Press, 2003).

Federal Census records, Productions of Agriculture Schedules. Available at Illinois State Archives, Springfield.

Federal Census records, Population Schedules. Those for Illinois available at Illinois State Archives, Springfield; those for Wisconsin available at the State Historical Society of Wisconsin, Madison. Also available in high-resolution digital format at www.ancestry.com.

Robert W. Finley, *Original Vegetation Cover of Wisconsin compiled from U. S. General Land Office Notes* (St. Paul, Minn.: North Central Forest Experiment Station, Forest Service, U.S. Department of Agriculture, 1976). Map, 1:500,000. Designed and prepared by the Cartography Laboratory, University of Wisconsin, Madison.

Government Land Office records. The land patents are available at www.glorecords.blm.gov. The survey plats for Wisconsin are available at same website. The survey plats of the Illinois lands of interest here are available at http://landplats.ilsos.net.

Talbot Hamlin, *Greek Revival Architecture in America: Being an account of important trends in American architecture and American life prior to the war between the states* (New York: Dover, 1964), p. 306. This edition is a reprinting of the 1944 publication by Oxford University Press.

William Henry Jennings, *A Genealogical History of the Jennings Families in England and America. In Three Volumes. Volume II The American Families* (Columbus, Ohio: Wann & Adair Press, 1899). Note: Volumes I and III were apparently never published.

Land Records. Stephenson County, Illinois. Available at: a) Recorder of Deeds, Stephenson Co., Freeport, Illinois; b) Stephenson County Abstracting Co., Freeport, Illinois.

Allen G. Noble, *Wood, Brick and Stone: The North American Settlement Landscape* (Amherst: University of Massachusetts Press, 1984).

Fred W. Peterson, *Homes in the Heartland: Balloon Frame Farmhouses of the Upper Midwest, 1850–1920* (Lawrence: University Press of Kansas, 1992).

H. Wayne Price and Keith A. Sculle, "Observations on the Pennsylvania German Barns in Stephenson County, Illinois," *Pioneer America Society Transactions* (vol. 8, 1985, p.45–53).

University of Wisconsin-La Crosse Murphy Library Special Collections, *Photograph* (cataloged as Farm Houses, Box #1, 19th C. Date: July 14, 1982. Donor: E. Hill. Neg. No.: 40647).

Wisconsin State Census of 1855. Available at the State Historical Society of Wisconsin, Madison.